Is He Straight?

Is He Straight?

The Checklist for
Women Who Wonder

Bonnie Kaye, M.Ed.

toExcel
San Jose New York Lincoln Shanghai

Is He Straight?

Published by toExcel
an imprint of iUniverse.com, Inc.

For information address:
iUniverse.com, Inc.
620 North 48th Street
Suite 201
Lincoln, NE 68504-3467
www.iuniverse.com

ISBN: 0-595-00439-3

Printed in the United States of America

Dedicated to:

My mother, who always believed in me,
The man in my life who made me believe in myself,
My Orleans friends, who encourage me daily,
And Luz who inspired me to find the courage.

Introduction

A woman enters into a marriage with the hopes, dreams, and plans of a happy and fulfilling life with the man with whom she intends to build a life and family. The central theme surrounding these aspirations is the one of honesty. When the man goes into the marriage with the same goals, but leaves out the honesty piece, the marriage is doomed for both parties and their future children.

Millions of women in this country unknowingly marry homosexual men only to learn at some point why their marriages are so difficult and problematic. In most cases, these men were aware of their homosexuality before the marriage, but were hoping for a "miracle" that would change them. Marriage would be the answer to those ever-present gnawing attractions to men that would mysteriously vanish by wishful thinking. Living the "straight life" could change their impulses towards men because their wives would fulfill their sexual needs.

There's no treachery intended here. Let's be logical. We are living in a society that will never accept homosexuality as "normal." Gay people are openly discriminated against and persecuted. They are looked at as being deviant, distorted, and perverted. Families, friends, and associates often cut them off once the truth is known. Isn't it worth taking the chance to change this if marriage might be the answer?

In these enlightened times, we still find an abundance of ignorance towards homosexuality. Gay people are killed and brutalized by homophobic mobs. The majority of the straight community still believes that "gay" is a choice that someone makes. But why would anyone consciously choose a lifestyle that is scorned by so many?

For approximately 25% of gay men, heterosexual sex is possible, even though it is not preferable. These men have the most difficult time coming to terms with their homosexuality because they can "perform" with a woman. They want the chance to live the American dream, but instead, in time, it becomes a nightmare. Two of the most difficult situations come into play—living a lie on a daily basis, and forcing yourself to be what you aren't and can't be—namely, straight.

The women who are faced with the truth, usually at the time when it becomes convenient for their husbands to reveal this information, feel trapped in their own personal "twilight zone." After they learn about their husbands' homosexuality, numerous questions arise with limited resources for finding the answers that make sense.

This book has been written to help straight women and gay men understand the dynamics of their marriages by answering the difficult questions that are so confusing. These are answers based on fifteen years of counseling thousands of women across this country who were in this position.

Unfortunately, there is no quick fix to alleviate the pain that each woman suffers, but this book will give insight into how and why this happens. Hopefully, you will find all of the answers you are looking for presently that will allow you to move towards a happier future.

Chapter 1

My Personal Story

On September 17, 1982, my husband, Michael, packed two suitcases and stormed out of our home. His parting words were, "I'll be staying with my family. I'll be back next week to pick up the rest of my things."

I watched him throw the luggage into the car and then pull away without turning back for a final glimpse. For a few minutes, I stared out the window, frozen in time. My mind came to a complete stop, but I was soon jolted by the screams of my three-month-old son, Alex. He sensed the tension that filled our home at that moment.

I picked up the baby, placed a bottle in his mouth, and started rocking him back and forth, cradled in my arms. I was too numb to cry, to talk, or even to whisper. I kept rocking the baby in a mechanical, steady rhythm, and I began to remember.

* * * * * * * * * * * * * * * * * *

In the spring of 1978, my life was at its best point ever. At the age of twenty-seven, I was the director of a major political organization headquartered in New York City. My job was challenging and very exciting. During that year, I traveled to fifteen cities around the country, appeared on national and local television programs, and interviewed with dozens of magazines and newspapers. I moved to New York from my home in Philadelphia after a year of exhausting commuting.

My personal life had changed dramatically for the better that year. Nine months earlier, I ended a three-year marriage to my first husband, Brad, who suffered from severe depression and anxiety. It was difficult living with a man who was mentally deteriorating week by week in spite of the forced psychotherapy (at my insistence) and the daily doses of antidepressants.

Physically, I temporarily conquered a chronic obesity problem that plagued me since childhood. For the first time as an adult, I looked attractive and felt wonderful about my life. Living in New York had been my dream since childhood, and now I had a chance to live out that dream. My life was almost complete—a great job, wonderful friends, and a nice apartment. The only thing missing was a man.

My attitude about men was typical of other women who grew up in what I refer to as the "Cinderella Era." I was born in 1951 when the social climate expected young women to marry shortly after high school or risk being labeled an "old maid." As a child, I was inspired by the fairy tales with the "happily ever after" endings. I was a gawky, overweight teenager whose ultimate goal was to find a loving man who would fall deeply in love with me and take care of my emotional need of being loved unconditionally.

In my desperate attempts to find this love, I began repeating a pattern of entering into destructive and disastrous relationships. My low self-esteem made me an easy target for men who were the takers in life, not the givers. Even though my first marriage failed, and in spite of other previous bad experiences, I was determined to find my soulmate.

When Michael walked into my office in June of 1978 asking to volunteer some of his time to our organization, I sensed there was something special about him. His charismatic nature, comedic wit, and handsome looks intrigued me. He was six feet tall with a shapely muscular body, long chestnut brown hair, and dark green eyes. There was an air of mystery about him that attracted me even more. I invited him to join me for dinner, and he graciously accepted.

We dined in a popular restaurant on the Lower East Side of New York and exchanged our life stories. Before I realized it, three hours had passed and the restaurant was closing. I apologized for taking up so much of Michael's time, but he said that it was the best evening he could ever remember.

As we parted, Michael promised to meet me at my office the next day after work. I went home thinking only of him. I had a strong premonition that this man would be my future husband. He had all of the qualities that I was looking for in a man—strength, intelligence, warmth, compassion, and humor.

Michael kept his word, and the following evening, appeared at my office. He offered to take me to a movie, but I was in the midst of a major advertising campaign and couldn't spare the time. He stayed in the office, making himself useful by answering telephones and greeting other volunteers. By 11:00 p.m., we called it a night and settled for a late night cup of coffee.

Michael and I started spending our free moments together, and several days later, I began falling in love with him. I had always been a romantic, and I convinced myself that our meeting was more than chance—it was destiny. On an impulse, I agreed to move into Michael's apartment four weeks later.

The idea of marriage came up in our early conversations, and once the words were spoken, it seemed to be the natural course to take. We picked a date three months later in September, and we quickly found a hotel for the affair. In the confusion of the wedding preparations, it was easy to overlook some of Michael's imperfections that were becoming more apparent. There were some inconsistencies about his life that I questioned, but I accepted his explanations, wanting to believe him and not the voice of reason in my head that kept saying, "Be careful."

For instance, shortly after we met, I visited Michael in his office. He was employed as an accountant for a small insurance firm. The mail clerk stopped by to chat with him, but Michael never introduced me. When I asked him why, he explained that the co-worker was gay and had a crush on him. Michael didn't want to hurt the clerk's feelings by telling him we were getting married. I thought this sounded strange, but I also knew that Michael was a compassionate person who cared about other people's feelings. He told me it was nothing to worry about. After all, it was the clerk's problem—he was the gay one, not Michael. I thought this was odd, but shrugged it off.

Over the next few weeks, Michael introduced me to his friends that he had had since childhood. They all seemed excited about our upcoming marriage; however, they unanimously displayed surprise. Several of them commented that they thought Michael would never get married. When I told Michael about these comments, he explained that he had always told his friends he was a "confirmed bachelor" until he met me. When I met the members of his family shortly afterwards, they acted equally surprised, but at the same time, they gave us their blessings.

Michael was a volunteer for a local organization that mentored teenagers who were at risk of dropping out of high school. There were usually four or five of these young men surrounding us who looked at Michael as their personal guru. All of them were from dysfunctional families. Some came from homes without a father, while others had parents who were unstable due to drug and alcohol addiction or mental illness.

Between Michael's job and volunteering three times a week, and my twelve hour workdays, we had little time to spend alone. There always seemed to be people surrounding us, but I convinced myself that this would change after we were married.

Three weeks before the wedding, my friend Zack called me at work and said it was important to talk to me privately. There was a sound of urgency in his voice, so I arranged to meet him later that morning. Zack told me he had a lengthy conversation with Michael the night before. He came to our apartment not knowing that I was still at work, and Michael invited him in for coffee. From the hour conversation they had, Zack believed Michael was "at least bisexual if not homosexual." As soon as the word "homosexual" was spoken, my stomach tightened and my heart started to palpitate. I angrily told Zack that he was mistaken—there was no way Michael could be gay. We had spent numerous nights together making love. Zack meekly apologized for upsetting me but refused to change his story. I asked him what Michael had said that could possibly make him draw this mistaken conclusion. Zack replied that Michael directly told him that he had gay encounters in the past and claimed there was nothing wrong with it.

I wanted to forget this conversation, but I wondered how Michael could tell this to someone who was like a younger brother to me and a close friend. I called Michael at work and told him I wanted to meet him for dinner that night somewhere quiet because I had something I wanted to discuss with him. He sounded worried and repeatedly asked me what was wrong, but I assured him that it was nothing important. I tried to hide the anger in my voice, but he instinctively knew that I was upset. I didn't want to forewarn Michael because I needed to see his facial expressions when I questioned him about his "confessions" to Zack.

Later that evening, we sat down to order dinner with the usual pleasantries, but now forced on my part. After ordering, I told Michael about my conversation with Zack and asked him for an explanation. His face became red and twisted with anger. He was so infuriated that I was afraid he would knock the table over. As I calmed him down, I told him that I wasn't making accusations—I just wanted to know why he would give someone the impression that he was gay.

Michael responded by saying that Zack had started to talk to him about a sexual problem he was having with his girlfriend. Michael could see that Zack was troubled and suspected that the problem might be homosexuality. He didn't want Zack to feel embarrassed, so to ease his discomfort and win his confidence, Michael told Zack that he, too, had engaged in homosexual experiences in the past. He said that he felt bad about "lying," but he wanted Zack to feel that he could relate to his problem. Michael begged me not to repeat this to Zack because it would mean that he betrayed my friend's confidence.

Even though the story was strange, I eagerly accepted Michael's explanation. I was in love, and my wedding day was only a few weeks away. I was not about to risk losing him because of the sexual problems of my friend, and I dismissed Zack's accusations. When Zack called me the next day, I thanked him and told him not to worry about it—everything was under control. We never discussed the conversation again, and Zack quietly disappeared from our lives.

Of course, once the thought of homosexuality was in my head, it was hard not to think about it, but I kept telling myself that I was being ridiculous. Over the years I had been friendly with a few gay men, and they certainly weren't interested in women or marriage. Michael and I had sexual relations two or three times a week, and although he wasn't an expert lover, he was typical of other men who didn't know everything that pleased a woman. This didn't indicate homosexuality—just inexperience.

Michael showed me pictures of women whom he recently dated, and he also had close women friends. Why would a gay man be involved with women? It didn't add up, so I started to feel better. The fact that there was nothing effeminate about Michael also helped ease my fears. He physically appeared to be a man of strength and was nothing like the weak and fragile images associated with homosexuality. I erased these thoughts from my mind and replaced them with our upcoming marriage.

The wedding day took place three months after we met. We had 150 guests who joined us to celebrate. It was a beautiful event, and I felt hopeful that our future would be as wonderful as the wedding. Neither one of us had the energy to think about anything sexual that evening, but we promised to make up for it the next day.

We left for Florida the next morning for a seven-day honeymoon. I was thrilled to be away from the crowds of people that surrounded both of our lives, but specifically the young men Michael played "Big Brother" to who constantly interrupted our free time together with visits and phone calls. Although Michael's volunteer commitment was officially two evenings a week and Sunday afternoon, some of the guys showed up almost every day. I asked Michael to limit these visits because we needed more private time alone, but he brushed me off by saying that I was "overreacting" or being "too possessive."

Our vacation gave us time to talk and to know each other better. During one of those conversations, Michael said he had done some things in the past that he wasn't proud of, but he did them to survive. I tried to get him to talk about these "things," but he refused. My past was far from unblemished, so I disregarded his confessions and wrote them off to his unstable past. Michael was adopted at birth by parents who were not equipped to raise children. His mother mentally and verbally berated him by calling him obscene names; his father physically abused him. That's why he claimed to be so devoted to troubled youth—he had been one of them. These stories of abuse made me love Michael even more because when he told them, he seemed so vulnerable reflecting the pain he had grown up with.

Every evening during our week away, we made love before going to bed, no matter how tired we were. Michael kept saying that he wanted this to be a week we'd always remember, at least sexually. Sometimes he made sure that I was satisfied, but other times, he pleased himself only, leaving me frustrated. On those occasions, he consoled me by promising to "make it up to me next time."

I have never been assertive sexually, and it was difficult to discuss my sexual needs. I felt it was humiliating to keep reminding Michael that sex was for two people's pleasure, not just for one. In the beginning, Michael was a willing sex partner, but he made it clear that certain things about sex were unpleasant for him. He believed that a woman could be satisfied strictly by the act of intercourse. After our first few encounters left me frustrated, I cautiously explained my need for other ways of sexual stimulation. Michael became defensive, claiming that every woman he had sex with in the past was satisfied with his lovemaking. To give credibility to my point, I provided him with several popular books on the market about women's sexual needs. He eventually conceded that each woman had different sexual desires when I read him selections to emphasize my point. After my campaign for sexual awareness, Michael tried to accommodate my needs at times, but he made it clear that he was doing it for me even though he didn't enjoy it.

This attitude prevailed throughout our marriage and took most of the pleasure out of having sex. I felt as if our sex life was regulated by the "orgasm bank." When Michael didn't bother to satisfy me, he would always say he "owed me one." This was balanced in his mind by the times he satisfied me, but was unable to reach an orgasm, which meant I "owed him one." His debits always outweighed his credits, but I became tired of complaining and keeping score.

When we returned from Florida, I resigned from my job. The position required ten to twelve hours of work a day and extensive traveling. I didn't want to start the marriage with those kinds of demands on my time. Although I firmly believed a new couple needed quality time alone together, Michael felt differently.

His group members invaded our home almost every evening for hours. I tried to be patient and understanding, but I resented it. They made me feel uncomfortable, as though I was intruding in my own home with my own husband. When I told Michael that I wanted him to put an end to this chaos, he yelled at me, stating that I was acting "pushy and possessive." I was constantly reminded that I was his wife—not his boss or mother.

I became depressed. We were living in a suburb of New York, far away from the friends I knew and the city that I loved. We moved there following the wedding because Michael started a new job, and this was a more convenient location. I felt an emptiness in my life when I left my job and friends, and the isolation only intensified the void. Overnight, I went from being a person of semi-celebrity status to the wife of a man I hardly knew. I remember walking in our door one day several weeks after our move and thinking to myself, "How did I get here? Six months ago I didn't know this man and now he is my husband." There were still the constant interruptions in our life, leaving little time to build a relationship.

I aired my view to Michael that a marriage needs time and work if it is to grow and survive. I went through a bitter divorce and knew how difficult marriage could be. Michael strongly disagreed—he believed that as long as two people loved each other, this was enough. I tried to win Michael over to my way of thinking, but he kept verbally beating me down with his tongue-lashings. I usually gave in just to keep the peace.

By the sixth month of marriage, our sex life deteriorated rapidly. I felt as though Michael were making love to me more out of obligation than desire. As the months wore on, the frequency continued to decrease. Our sexual activity was reduced to once or twice a month.

When the pattern of diminishing sex started, I spoke to Michael about it. He replied that we were no longer newlyweds, and that married couples don't have sex all of the time. He suggested that something might be wrong with me—perhaps I was a "nymphomaniac." I snapped back that wanting to make love with my husband two or three times a week did not classify me as a sex maniac, but Michael ignored my words. On several occasions, when I brought up our sex life, he became defensive, saying that his lack of interest was due to various pressures, such as financial problems. At other times, he lashed out at me, claiming that my pushiness was a "turn-off" to him. It was difficult for me to think that wanting to make love with my husband was "pushy," but psychologically, his rejection took its toll on me. By the end of our first year of marriage, I learned to keep the thoughts about sex to myself, not wanting to turn Michael off more than he already was.

Between the lack of privacy in our home and the lack of intimacy in our bedroom, I became more depressed. Michael found quality time for everyone else in his life, from the members of his group to his family. Their problems always became his priorities. When I brought up the idea of marriage counseling, he refused to consider it. He claimed that if there were problems in our marriage, they were my problems. He was content in the marriage and didn't need counseling.

At the end of our first year of marriage, we moved to an apartment closer to the city. The move seemed to do miracles for our marriage. Michael became attentive to me for the first time since our courtship, and I felt that our marriage was becoming solid.

Our sex life didn't improve, but I hoped that it would if given some time. "Don't push," I told myself. "It will happen on its own with time." People often commented that the first year of marriage is the most difficult, and I was determined to make our second year a better one.

What really made me optimistic was the news I learned a week before our anniversary—I was pregnant! We were so excited, each for different reasons. Michael's family life had been unstable and having children represented the security and sense of belonging that he wanted. He was never able to accept the rejection of being given up at birth for adoption. Michael believed a child would be someone who belonged to him. He wanted the chance to give his own child the love and security he missed growing up.

I desperately wanted a child because I thought it would bond our marriage and give Michael the stability he needed. I thought that a baby would change Michael's need for his group and instead allow him to focus his energies on his family.

Two months before the baby's birth, I convinced Michael to move from New York to my hometown of Philadelphia. My family lived there, and I wanted to be near them when the baby arrived. This would be the first grandchild in our family, and I wanted my mother and younger sisters to be able to enjoy the baby. I also knew that a hundred-mile move would end the continuing intrusions we had from Michael's youth group members.

For the next few months, I felt that my decision to get married paid off. Michael treated me with the love and affection that had attracted me to him when we first met. I knew how important the baby was to him because he was willing to uproot his life in New York and move away from all that was important to him.

Part of his change in attitude for the better was also the fact that our sex life was non-existent during my pregnancy. I had some early complications, and we both decided not to take a chance of a miscarriage by any sexual stimulation. This took the pressure off Michael. When our daughter, Stephanie, was born in 1980, I felt our family was complete, and I was finally at peace.

Michael was a doting father from the first day. He would rush home after work to feed Stephanie and rock her to sleep in his arms singing lullabies. Michael went to bed early so he could take care of her 6:00 a.m. feedings before going to work. He carried her pictures everywhere and brought home a new toy every day for months.

Unfortunately, my false sense of security diminished as the months went on. Michael was overly gregarious, and within a short time, he became the local pied piper and attracted a small group of local troubled teenagers to mentor. Several of his New York members started coming in on Sunday mornings and stayed for the day, invading our new home. Once again, I started to feel like I was living in a teen-age youth center.

Michael made sure to distance the members of his group from me, forbidding them to tell me anything discussed during their sessions. If I asked them how the meetings went, they made it clear that they were not allowed to give any information to "outsiders." They were polite, but made me feel unwelcome in my own home.

Michael's new group consisted of adolescents in their late teens. They all had certain characteristics in common, such as a lack of self-confidence, unstable family lives, poor grades in school, no concrete future aspirations, and an unwavering state of devotion to Michael. I started to view this group as a mini-cult because Michael was involved in all decision-making in their lives. Even though Michael was an excellent mentor, it didn't seem reasonable for them to be this dependent on their leader.

Some of the member's families were annoyed because they seemed to have lost control over their own children. Michael wasn't fazed by the criticisms. He justified it by stating that the parents were to blame for the problems that were there. He believed he was changing their lives in a positive direction because he was able to give them the care and guidance their parents didn't give them. Part of Michael's success was making these teens feel as though each one was the most important part of Michael's life. He spent hours with each one, individually and in the group, talking about life, philosophy, and future career goals. The only thing he asked for in return was loyalty. Michael made the rules, and anyone who questioned them was immediately dismissed. When Michael dismissed a member of the group, the other members also had to turn their backs on him.

By the time of our second anniversary, our life was more chaotic than ever. Michael started a retail clothing business and used the group members to help him run it. Between the business and his volunteer work, our home was constantly overrun with intruders again. When they weren't there in person, they were on the phone or in our discussions and arguments.

At times when my frustration became overwhelming, I would sob hysterically. Michael became alarmed and the daily visits would temporarily stop. But within a few days, they gradually started again always with some excuse of urgency. Before long, things were back to abnormal. I was not strong enough to give Michael an ultimatum. During our arguments, he was clear that if I made him choose between his life or our life, our family life would lose. Michael claimed that he would never allow anyone to control his life or tell him what he could or couldn't do. No one had that right, not even his wife. The fact that his activities controlled my life was no concern to him.

I tried to analyze Michael's need for this adoration by others and concluded that he needed to overcome his own insecurities by elevating himself to a role that people admired and looked up to. I worked to overcompensate in our marriage by giving in to almost every demand, hoping that someday my love and acceptance would suffice. I was only kidding myself. On some level, I knew it was a losing battle, but I refused to accept it.

In the later part of our second year of our marriage, a young man, Jimmy, joined Michael's group and became a constant visitor in our home. Even though he was almost 18 years old, he refused to make any decision in his life without consulting Michael. Jimmy scared me because his behavior was typical of the cult mentality. He had a glazed blank look in his eyes, and his speech pattern was monotone and deliberate. Michael was spending more time than usual with Jimmy and laughed at my warnings about his mental state. He bragged that since Jimmy joined the group, he left the delinquent crowd he had been part of and stopped taking drugs. When I pointed out that Jimmy had replaced this with an obsession for Michael, he shrugged it off and told me that I was imagining things. Jimmy gave me a very eerie feeling. There were days I would look out my window and see him standing there just staring. Michael blamed me claiming that I caused this by not allowing him in the house whenever he wanted to visit.

Four months after I started complaining about Jimmy, Michael started acting differently. After several nights of restless sleeping, pacing back and forth, and unresponsive conversation, I asked him what was bothering him. I assured Michael that he could discuss anything with me without my getting upset. He was still reluctant, but finally started to talk.

He told me that I was right about Jimmy and his obsession for Michael. He decided he had to do something because Jimmy had become much too dependent on him. I felt a strong sense of relief that Michael finally saw things from my perspective. I told him that the only logical solution was to ask Jimmy to leave the group. Michael said this was impossible to do. He started to list a number of reasons why, such as his concern that Jimmy would go back to drugs and destroy his life. He then casually threw in that something had happened between them during a "moment of weakness." He kept on talking as if nothing out of the norm had been said, but I no longer heard the words he was speaking. I felt a strange fuzziness in my head as if someone had just hit me with a hard object. After that moment passed, I asked Michael what he meant by a "moment of weakness." He refused to reveal any details, assuring me that it was nothing to get upset about. I asked the question again, but Michael told me that my imagination was playing tricks on me.

I stayed awake that night, trying to understand what was going on. If nothing had actually happened between them, then why was Michael so afraid to break his ties with Jimmy? He did tell me that he was afraid that Jimmy might go to his parents and they could "misinterpret" the story, making it into something that it wasn't. He said that he had to keep seeing Jimmy because this was the only way he had some control over the situation.

I pieced together different incidents that made me uneasy during our marriage and a picture began to form. I remembered

Michael's statements about having to survive by doing unmentionable things he wasn't proud of. He always quickly added that he did these acts as a teenager and only for money, so I didn't dwell on it. Several times when we were having financial problems, Michael mentioned that he could earn money quickly by dancing in clubs. When he added that it would be an all-male club, I angrily told him it was out of the question. I assumed or maybe hoped this was what he alluded to in his past that he wasn't proud of, but now I wasn't so sure. Other hints started running through my mind.

When we lived in New York City, we often dined in a restaurant located in the gay section of Greenwich Village. Michael told me he spent a lot of time in this area when he was younger. Once we went to a movie theater in that neighborhood, and we were the only male-female couple there. All of the other patrons were men, and many of them were gay couples openly displaying affection. I felt uncomfortable there, especially when some of them were eyeing Michael up and down. When I expressed my discomfort, Michael said I was paranoid. After all, he was a married man and wore a wedding ring to prove it.

Michael pampered himself and looked into the mirror countless times, admiring his good looks. He often remarked that gay men would tell him how handsome he was, and if a gay man says it, you know it is true because they only complimented good-looking men. I thought this was odd, but I assumed his ego needed constant reassurance, and he was not fussy about the source of compliments.

Michael would throw "gay" into our conversations frequently, whether as a joke, an observation of a stranger, or a mocking imitation of the stereotypical movements of an effeminate male's hands and walk. One day we passed a blond teenage boy riding a bicycle, and Michael explained that in the gay world, the boy would be called a "cutie pie." He was annoyed when different co-workers occasionally asked him if he was gay, and he always let them know that he was a married man with a child. However, I remembered the famous quote about protesting too much. I started to feel that my daughter and I were a shield for his denials when someone made this accusation.

When I thought about all these things combined with my friend Zack's warning before the marriage, I concluded that my husband had homosexual tendencies, and might, in fact, be "bisexual."

The next day, I sat Michael down for a talk and stated that I thought he might be bisexual. I didn't ask him directly because I knew he would lie. After the words were spoken, there was neither confirmation nor denial. I quickly added that I could accept that he had "bisexual tendencies." In fact, if once every six months or so he had to go away for a few hours, and I would never have to find out about it, I could live with the situation. And if, by chance, I did find out, I only hoped it would be with a consenting adult and not a teenager. I had the situation all wrapped up neatly under acceptable terms that I could live with. I became sick to my stomach when I visualized Michael with another man, but I was counting on never finding out if it happened.

I understood very little about homosexuality. If I had known more, I would have realized how ridiculous and unrealistic my terms and conditions were. I should have considered that Michael's approval of this plan was just a tactic to placate me while giving him the green light to continue cheating on me.

I also demanded that Jimmy be removed from our lives, no matter what the consequences were. It was Michael's word against his, and who would believe an unstable teenager over a married man and father? Michael finally agreed, and I started to feel as if I could still hold the marriage together and survive emotionally. I also thought that my extreme generosity would make Michael love me more.

The next few months were calmer. Michael assured me that Jimmy was gone, and he made a sincere effort to keep the other group members out of our personal life. He moved their sessions out of our home and into the store we rented. This made my life much easier because the group had outgrown our home, and I was forced to leave it whenever the meetings took place. This put added strain on me, and made me feel like an outsider in my own home.

Michael started talking about having another child, claiming that a son would be the fulfillment of his lifetime dream and change his focus. He never explained what he meant by his "focus," but I assumed that he meant he would cut down on the time he spent with his group and his "bisexual thoughts." In my desperate attempts to make my marriage work, I manipulated our limited sexual activity to my most fertile days.

A month before our third anniversary, I conceived, but I had mixed feelings. After the initial excitement wore off, I didn't feel the same sense of joy that I had with my first child. Early in the pregnancy, Michael became involved with someone he hired named John who was 19 years old. When I confronted him with my suspicions, he claimed once again that I was crazy and paranoid. By then, I was familiar with his behavior patterns and knew something was going on between them. When I watched Michael get dressed up and put on expensive cologne when he went out, I knew he was feeling an attraction.

On the evening of our third anniversary, Michael told me that he had to do something important and would be home shortly. I prepared a special dinner that sat warming in the oven until he quietly unlocked the door at 3:00 a.m. I was sitting on the living room couch staring blankly at the walls. I didn't say a word while I listened to his explanation. Michael coldly stated that he was trying to find a place for John to stay because he had been kicked out of his house for doing drugs. Michael had the gall to blame me for his absence on our anniversary because I refused to allow John to stay with us.

Up until this point, I never threw the issue of homosexuality in Michael's face, but now I found myself bringing it up in every argument. I distrusted him so much that I suspected him of doing wrong daily even when he wasn't. I began watching the clock every time he left the house, calculating the minutes until he returned. I searched his pockets when he slept, hoping to find evidence to confirm my suspicions. I became a person totally alien even to myself. The worst part was knowing that I was too weak to do anything even if I did find proof.

What I originally saw as strength in Michael was a misconception. He used his strength to bully me, mentally beating me down through verbal abuse. He robbed me of my self-esteem that took years to build up by berating me privately and publicly. He kept telling me that without him, I could never survive alone, and eventually I started to believe that I was helpless. He criticized me daily, finding fault with my parenting skills, housekeeping, family, and friendships. I began to eat to compensate for my unhappiness, and as I gained weight, he said that my size was the cause of his lack of sexual interest. He repeated over and over that no man would ever love me as much as he did, and without him, I would be condemned to a life of loneliness.

I became a prisoner of my own insecurities. I was afraid to leave my home, fearing Michael would bring someone into my bed. Friends who had known me for years questioned what was happening to me. I told my family and closest friends about the problems, and although they were sympathetic, they didn't really understand the situation or have any answers. Michael did his best to distance me from the people I was closest to at the time by starting fights with me in front of them and making them choose sides. My family and friends stopped coming over and instead met me away from home on those rare occasions when I left the house. Michael strongly warned me that he would leave if he ever found out that I discussed his secret with anyone. This included talking to a marriage counselor, even though I pleaded with him to go with me for help. He also threatened that he would not leave alone—he would take the children and I would never see them. With nowhere to turn and living with constant fear, I was left to deal with our problems alone.

When our son, Alex, was born in June of 1982, we were in a state of financial disaster. Our business was quickly going bankrupt, and there was virtually no cash flow coming in. This put additional strain on our marriage, making each day unbearable. I still had moments when strong feelings of love would surface, but they quickly faded underneath my stronger feelings of resentment and hatred. I also despised myself for being too weak to take any positive action. Michael and I had little communication except when we had to discuss something about the children or the business. Most of our conversations were in the form of an argument.

Our marriage had become one of existence—there was no tenderness, intimacy, laughter, or friendship. Our sex life was non-existent, which was fine with me. There was no way I could be aroused by a man who was making my life a living hell. I started to fantasize about ways to kill Michael because I didn't see any way out of the marriage if he was alive. Although it is easy for others to judge a situation and say "walk away," for the person living it day to day, it is never that simple.

Three months after Alex was born, and two weeks before our fourth anniversary, things came to a head. One evening when Michael went to sleep, I saw his wallet sitting on the kitchen table. There was a lined piece of paper conspicuously sticking out. I removed it. When I opened the paper, I saw it was a letter and my eyes immediately skipped down to the signature, which read, "Love, Jimmy." As I went to the top, I read the words that gave me the proof I'd been waiting for. The letter stated that Jimmy still loved Michael even though he had chosen to stay in the marriage. There were two recent occasions mentioned when the two of them had been together even though Michael swore to me that he had never heard from Jimmy again.

After reading the letter, I ran to the bathroom to vomit. When I finished, I woke Michael up and confronted him with the letter. He became enraged and shouted that I had no business reading his private mail, and he was sick of my invasion of his privacy. I told him that I was not giving in this time. He could no longer continue to lie to me and expect me to accept it. He claimed nothing had happened between him and Jimmy, and their encounters had been only by chance. I wanted to believe him, but I could no longer live in a state of denial.

For the next two weeks, we fought constantly, calling each other terrible names and making terrible accusations. Finally, after one very heated argument, Michael packed his bags and left for New York. The marriage was over.

Michael returned a week later with his suitcases in hand, knocking at the door. He decided "to give me one more chance." By this time, it was too late. During the one week of his absence, my mental strength had returned, and I told him that he was not welcome back. Michael was in shock and didn't believe it. He asked me if I was willing to break up a family for my own selfish reasons, and I said, "Yes, yes, yes!"

Chapter 2

Questions Most Asked by Straight Wives about their Gay Husbands

During the last fifteen years, I have counseled over 5,000 women who either are or have been married to gay men. I have compiled a list of the questions that are most commonly asked. After reading the answers, you will gain a better insight into the situation.

Q. What is your definition of a "gay" man?

A. I define a man as gay if he fits into any of these categories:

a. He is presently engaging in extramarital relations with another male.

b. He has had sex with a male on more than one occasion since his marriage, assuming he had no previous sexual contact with males prior to the marriage.

      c.   He was involved in a gay relationship prior to the time of marriage other than adolescent experimentation.

      d.   He has not yet acted on his feelings; however, he is discussing the desire to engage in homosexual behavior.

It is quite common for males to experiment sexually with other males at some point in their lives, usually during adolescence. If, however, this need for "experimentation" develops at a later age, it does not necessarily denote homosexuality.

After one homosexual encounter, a male may still be confused about his sexual orientation. Perhaps he was nervous and this inhibited his enjoyment. However, by the second or third time, he should have an idea of whether or not gay sex is gratifying or enjoyable for him. By the fourth or fifth encounter, it is no longer an experiment, but rather a preference.

Married men who suddenly express a desire to try gay sex may have been suppressing their needs until that time. That desire was always present even if it had not been acted on. Those men were hoping that marriage would be the "miracle cure" that would make them "normal," but looking back they admit those feelings of attraction for men were always present.

     Q.   **My husband still has sexual relations with me. Doesn't that make him bisexual, rather than gay?**

     A.   Bisexuality is a controversial issue, and there are numerous definitions of this word. I have yet to meet the man who is truly bisexual in the sense that he does not have a sexual preference.

Just because a gay man has sexual relations with a woman, that in and of itself does not mean that he is bisexual. It means that he can *perform* heterosexual sex. Some men perform out of duty, others out of an emotional need, and still others because they need a sexual release and their wives are handy. These men can complete sex, orgasm (sometimes), and a few even feel satisfied, but they still would prefer to have sex with a male partner.

Often, the gay husband and the straight wife use the term "bisexual" because it is easier to deal with emotionally. It is more acceptable in our homophobic society and justifies a reason for keeping a marriage together. It is difficult for both partners to come to terms with homosexuality, and the classification of "bisexual" postpones the inevitable of dealing with the issue. I address the issue of bisexuality in Chapter 9 of this book.

Q.   Why is my husband gay?

A.   There are various theories about why a person is gay, but none has been proven completely. Some say genetics, while others say environmental factors. I believe that homosexuality is determined before birth. I have seen families where there are five children and one is gay, or four children and two are gay. If environment is the main factor, why aren't all of the children gay?

Some people say that homosexuality is caused by a domineering mother and a passive father, claiming the father is a poor role model. Others say this occurs in families where the mother is passive and the father is aggressive and a poor role model. Almost everyone has one of these parent combinations, and yet, most of society is not homosexual. Although environment may have some effect, it is unlikely to determine a person's sexual preference.

An example that challenges the environmental theory focuses on men who are in prisons. It is quite common for men who are straight to participate in gay sex while they are confined for a long period of time with no access to women, even though they had never considered homosexual relations prior to imprisonment. When these men are released from prison, they resume sexual relations with women without giving a thought to returning to gay sex. Even though they actively participated in homosexuality for long periods of time because of environmental factors, their basic sexual instincts did not change.

Q.   Didn't my husband know he was gay before he got married?

A.   Chances are he did know, but like you, he was misinformed. He thought that as long as he could "perform" with a woman, he was really straight. Most likely, he had one or more gay encounters with little success and/or lots of guilt and concluded that the straight world was where he belonged.

I have met gay men who insisted they didn't know for sure that they were gay until after their marriages. But, even though this discovery came late, these men knew that there was something different about their sexuality, even if they didn't pinpoint their feelings as homosexual.

Q.   Why would a person who knows he is gay want to marry?

A.   Gay men marry for a variety of reasons. The most common reason is because they are hoping for a miracle "cure" that will make them straight. Gay men who can function sexually with women (approximately 25%) often feel that their sexual desire for men will diminish once they are married and domestically settled. Marriage provides the illusion of heterosexuality, but it is only temporary. Within a short time, the husband realizes that his sexual urges for men are just as strong as ever, and the excitement he feels for his wife can never compare to the excitement he feels about men.

Other gay men marry because they have been brought up with the same American dream as straight men—the loving wife and the children in the house with the picket fence. For younger men in their twenties and thirties, the gay world often proves frustrating or empty. This results in the American dream looking better and better, causing gay men to convince themselves that they are ready to "give up the gay life and go straight."

Another reason gay men marry is their desire to have children. Though paternal feelings can be genuine, fatherhood also creates a safe family unit and proves one's masculinity to the outside world.

Gay men also marry because marriage provides a cover in today's homophobic society. Many high-level jobs would not promote a person to a higher level if homosexuality was suspected. Marriage and the family is a perfect cover and it allays the fears of the suspicious.

The ability to sexually function with a woman prompts some gay men (about 25%) into marriage because in this situation they can cling to the illusion that they are straight. These are the men I feel most sorry for. They are neither here nor there, fish nor fowl, caught in between two worlds, neither of which they feel completely comfortable in. In most cases, they do not find sustained happiness in their lives because of their inability to come to terms with themselves.

I have also met men who deny their homosexuality for years, even though they have regular homosexual encounters. I have questioned these men about how they can deny this side of themselves, but they honestly can't come to terms with it. They need to believe they are straight to such a degree that they deny their gayness altogether.

> Q. Since my husband can function sexually in a heterosexual manner why does he "choose" the gay lifestyle?

A.   This is a statement that I often hear from straight people—"It's his choice to be gay. He doesn't have to be if he doesn't want to be. After all, he's married (or has been married) and has children!"

When you think about this statement, you'll realize how ridiculous it is. Why would anyone "choose" to be gay? Why would someone consciously choose to be part of a world that is frequently viewed by society as deviant or perverted? Why would anyone risk losing his family, home, job, and reputation if given a choice?

I surveyed 350 gay men and asked all of them the same question: "If you could take a pill tonight that would make you straight by morning, would you take it?" I received a resounding "yes" from 337 of those surveyed. Ten of them were not sure, and three said no. The overwhelming response came not out of shame, but out of a sense of reality. The world has not accepted homosexuality, and the gay lifestyle is not an easy one. How much simpler life would be for these men, if only they were straight.

A person does not "choose" his sexuality any more than he chooses his race or height. Once someone is gay, regardless of how he became gay, that is his orientation. A person can suppress or repress his sexual preference for indefinite periods of time, but eventually, in most cases, learns to come to terms with his true self.

> **Q.**   **Can my husband's homosexuality be helped through some kind of therapy?**
>
> **A.**   *No!* Many men spend years of their lives and

waste thousands of dollars looking for a "cure" that does not exist. There are groups such as "Homosexuals Anonymous" that convince gay men that they can change if their belief in God is strong enough. "Aversion therapy" is a treatment that shows films to gay men that are meant to turn them away from their inborn orientation. These tactics may cause a temporary shift in sexual practices, but they by no means change the person's homosexual desire.

The mind is a powerful tool, and a person can talk himself into another state of mind. However, somewhere down the line, a person's natural orientation will surface.

There are people who insist that God, therapy, or other miracles are the solution. However, I question the quality of life of someone who has to live being something he is not. Is it fair to a person to have to change his personality or orientation just to conform to the rules or beliefs of society? How happy can that person be if he can't be himself and has to be constantly on guard to hide his natural inclinations and feelings?

Gay men who suppress their sexuality to pass in the straight world often become mentally and/or physically abusive to their wives. They blame their wives, their closest and most convenient target, for forcing them to live a lie, even when the wife is clueless to her husband's homosexuality. Obviously, this is no way for a marriage to exist.

> **Q.** My husband claims that he has not acted on his homosexuality for two (five, ten, etc.) years. Is it possible that he is over it?

A. A man does not "get over" his homosexuality. He may be sincere and honest in his belief that he is no longer gay, but the fact remains that a person's sexual orientation does not change.

In an effort to save their marriage, position, respectability, etc., some men make a valiant effort to change and repress their sexual desires for an indefinite amount of time. Eventually, those feelings surface, and the problem must be faced again.

Often, gay men who are married will tell their wives, "It's over, I got it out of my system," or "I've outgrown those feelings," or "I was just experimenting," or "It was just a sexual impulse, but now it's over and I'm ready to be a good husband." Although these words may be sincerely meant when spoken, they are not realistic. The wife is so desperate to resolve the problem that she believes and accepts these explanations. Unfortunately, it is just a temporary reprieve. Within time, the pattern will recur, and the wife will be back where she started, with more years wasted on an impossible dream.

Q.   My husband insists that if I had been a better (more attractive, more supportive, less demanding, etc.) wife, he would not have turned to someone of the same sex. Is this true?

A.   *Absolutely not.* Your husband was gay long before both of you ever met. His conscious attraction for men may not have surfaced until after your marriage, but it was there, either suppressed or denied.

Due to the difficulty of accepting homosexuality within himself, the gay husband will often blame his wife for his sexual orientation. This practice of shifting blame is one of the ways wives of gay men become mentally beaten down and lose their self-esteem. What can be more psychologically damaging than thinking you are responsible for your husband's turning to other men? This head game is usually quite successful because most women don't understand homosexuality. They think that just because their husbands married them and that they had sex that produced children, they are straight.

All of a sudden, it "appears" as if the husband is losing his sexual desire for his wife, as his desire for men is increasing. What the wife doesn't know is that her husband's need for men was always greater than his need for her, and that his sexual desire for his wife was much more emotional than physical.

Ironically, if there is a common personality trait among wives of gay men, it is the fact that they are usually more supportive and understanding while being less demanding than other women. This is what attracts gay men to them—their belief that their wives' accepting personalities will extend to their hidden homosexuality if the truth does get out.

Wives of gay men come in all different shapes, sizes, colors, and nationalities. The average woman who marries a gay man looks the same as the average woman who marries a straight man. Even if the wife looks like Miss America, she can never be attractive enough to change her husband's proclivity. Women simply have the wrong "plumbing," and that's all there is to it!

> Q.   Why did my husband choose to tell me about his homosexuality at this particular point in our marriage?

A.   There is no set time when a man decides to reveal this information to his wife. Some men come out within the first year of marriage, while other men wait until their 25th wedding anniversary or even later. A husband's decision to come out is usually based on at least one of the following factors:

1. He gets tired of living a lie and coping with the guilt.
2. He has met a man with whom he wants to have a relationship.
3. He is ready to leave the marriage and is strong enough to tell his wife the truth.
4. He has acted on his gay sexual needs and now is finally sure about his sexuality and doesn't want to hide it.
5. He is going through mid-life crisis and changes.
6. He has experienced the death of a close loved one.

In most of the cases that I know, the husband comes out at his convenience, not at the wife's, and this is usually at a time when he doesn't care whether or not his wife will accept his being gay. In most cases, he has met someone and wants to start a relationship with him. Or he becomes mentally and emotionally strong enough to become part of the gay world.

There are women who have told me, "He shouldn't have told me when he did—it wasn't a good time." Let's be honest, could there ever be a good time to hear this news? Of course not. This news is devastating no matter when you hear it. The sooner you learn about your husband's homosexuality, the better it is for you. Think of all of the women who never find out what is wrong in their marriage and go through life thinking there is something wrong with them. It is better to find out too soon than too late, and no matter when you find out, it isn't soon enough.

> Q.   I have been told that it was impossible for me not to know that my husband was gay before we were married, and that subconsciously, I must have wanted to marry a gay man. Is this possible?
>
> A.   I hear gay men use this reason as an excuse for why it was okay not to inform their wives, but I don't believe this is true overall. In most instances, it is impossible to know ahead of time that a spouse is gay, especially if he is making every effort to hide it. Some women have told me that they were drawn to their husbands because they were nurturing, caring, and affectionate. They appreciated the fact that their spouse wasn't looking to jump into sexual relations immediately like many men are. Other women had limited experiences with men, and even if they thought something was not quite right, they didn't understand what it could be. Most straight women have very limited experiences with gay men. Why would they think that a gay man

would want to or even be able to have a relationship with a straight woman? For the small number of women that I have spoken to who knew that their husbands were gay prior to marriage (approximately 5%), most believed that marriage would change their husband's sexual orientation.

I have spoken to some women who are afraid to get involved in a relationship again because they are convinced that somehow, on a subconscious level, they will be attracted to another gay man. If this starts to become a pattern, it is certainly worth looking into through personal counseling. But most women will be cautious in their approach to dating and have a better idea of what to look for in a partner.

> Q.   My husband feels that since he can be honest with himself about his sexuality, he'd like to be honest with our children. I am not comfortable with this. How do I handle this?
> A.   This problem occurs in most families, and the answer is complex. The most important issue to focus on is the welfare of the child or children. Any decision that is made should be thought out with the best interests of the children in mind. Often, children are caught up in the battles of the parents' morals and egos, and they come out the losers.

How your child reacts to this news will depend on several factors:

1. Age—If a child is too young to comprehend the concept of sexuality, it can be damaging to discuss this. If a child is nearing adolescence, it is advisable not to reveal this information. For teenagers, sexuality is such a sensitive issue that this piece of information can definitely confuse the teenager even more. It

causes the child to start questioning his/her own sexuality and feel an added burden.

2. Location of residency—If you live in an area that is very conservative, church-oriented, or far away from a large metropolitan city, chances are that the community will not be too accepting of homosexuality in general. Local attitudes definitely influence the way a child thinks. In large cities where gay communities are more visible and people tend to be more accepting in their attitudes in general, there is a better chance for your child to feel more comfortable about this because chances are the gay father may feel more comfortable.

3. Relationship between father and child—If a father has a close, nurturing relationship with his child(ren), the news will be easier to accept, especially if the father plans to continue the family relationship in the same vein. If the father has been aloof, abusive, uncaring, uncommunicative, etc., his homosexuality is just one more disappointment.

4. Relationship between the parents:

(a) If living together—If both parties have come to terms with this situation and decided to deal with it as best as they can, fighting and hostilities should be at a minimum. But if either partner resents being in the marriage and conflicts are a common event, the child will blame homosexuality for the unrest in his/her home.

(b) If living apart—I always say that when children are involved, you are tied together for life, so it is preferable to be friends rather than enemies for the sake of the children. If both parents have an understanding of each other's values and put the welfare of the child before personal desires, pleasures, or judgments, the child will have an easier time accepting the gay parent. If the straight mother condemns, downgrades, criticizes, ridicules or calls the father names, it will be difficult for the child to have positive feelings about the gay parent.

Much of this depends on the next issue:

5. How the gay father handles his sexuality—I do not feel there is any reason for a parent to behave in a way that makes his child uncomfortable. If a child cannot deal with the father's homosexuality, then he/she should not be exposed to the father's gay lover(s), organizations, or hangouts. Homosexuality may be a lifestyle, but it is one that does not have to be displayed publicly. Fathers who constantly shove their homosexuality at their children are not helping them accept the situation, but rather turning them off even more.

It is important for the child to be given the time he/she needs to adjust to this situation while at the same time, to receive positive reinforcement from both parents. If a child does not accept the situation, the father should not take the attitude of, "Well, the hell with him/her, it's my life and I'll do what I want. After all, he's/she's only a kid." That attitude will hinder any chance for a positive father-child relationship. The father should send the child cards or letters that reassure his love and availability. When a child does start spending time with his father again, the father should do everything possible to make sure that it is quality father/child time—not father, child and lover or other friends. Be aware of the child's needs. Remember, it took the father a long time to accept his own homosexuality; the child may also need a long period of time to deal with it.

> Q.   If my husband is gay, is there any greater chance that my child or children will be gay?

A.   This is a difficult question to answer because there is not enough scientific information on this. Statistically, it is said that 10% of the general population is gay. From several limited studies that I have seen over the years, statistics state that the number of children born gay with one gay parent is between 10% and 18%. It is not unusual for children of gay parents to question their sexuality more frequently than other children. Whether or not this is cause for concern has not been scientifically researched enough to make any concrete conclusions. However, if you believe the theory as I do about homosexuality being genetic, it would only follow that the chances of having a gay child are definitely higher.

Q.   In desperately trying to keep my marriage together, I have tried to be open minded by reading books about homosexuality, going to gay bars, and going to meetings with other couples in the same situation. After a year of trying to relate, I am less comfortable than ever and thinking of divorce. Do you think I need more time to adjust or that I am not open minded enough?

A.   It is not uncommon for some women to do everything possible to try to understand their husbands' homosexual world, including being part of it. During the first year that I started my support group, I spent a significant amount of time learning about the gay community. I felt it was unfair to talk about gay issues unless I understood what they were really about.

After a year of "relating," I removed myself from the gay scene because I found myself getting depressed. I was constantly reminded of the horrors of my own marriage, and I kept reliving parts of my nightmare every time I went into a gay club or meeting. Although I did gain a valuable education about gay lifestyles, mentalities, and values, my advice to women who think that joining in on their husbands' lifestyle may help their marriage is: *don't do it!*

The more time you spend in this world that is not yours, the more confused, depressed, and demoralized you will become. There is nothing wrong with feeling uncomfortable about homosexuality—*especially when it is part of your marriage!* No matter how open and accepting we are of others and what they choose to do in their lives, the situation becomes quite different once it is forced onto us and into *our* lives. Homosexuality is a way of life that is acceptable to those who are homosexual, but not for those who are not. Your gay husband has no choice in his homosexuality, but you have even less to say about it.

Even women who find themselves accepting of gay people, and, in fact, have gay friends, are confused by their inability to cope with their husband's homosexuality. Don't fall into this trap. Accepting a stranger's homosexuality or even a friend's does not have a direct effect on your life. Having a gay husband does. You are suddenly thrust into a world that most of us have grown up to believe is amoral, distorted, and taboo. You now visualize your partner for life wrapped in the arms of another man. Some women cannot picture what goes on past that point, but even this limited image is enough to bring on a feeling of heartbreak and revulsion.

Finding out that a spouse is unfaithful with a woman is difficult enough to deal with under ordinary circumstances. Finding out that your spouse is making love to a man is more than most women can cope with. It is ridiculous to think that there is something wrong with you because you are not comfortable with the gay world. Some husbands will try to make their wives feel guilty by telling them about other wives who are accepting of their husbands' homosexuality, and who, in fact, even accompany their husbands to gay bars and outings. Be aware that this is the exception—not the norm. Some women will take desperate measures to save or hold their marriages or hold onto their husbands.

There are a small percentage of women who claim not to be bothered by their husband's sexuality and even go so far as to state that they can deal with another man, but not another woman. Some gay fathers' or gay husbands' organizations will use these women as propaganda to convince other women that having a gay husband is no big deal. *Don't be misled.* It is a *very big deal,* and a woman with a healthy thinking mind will not stay married to a gay man indefinitely.

> Q. I have been divorced from my gay husband for two years and almost all aspects of my life have gotten back to normal except for one—sex. For some reason, I just can't resume sexual relations. I freeze up as soon as I get close to someone. Is this unusual?
>
> A. It is very common for women who have had gay husbands to have sexual hang-ups for short or long periods of time after the marriage. During the marriage, a wife is often faced with feelings of inadequacy because her husband does not want her. The sexual patterns of straight couples are considered "abnormal" by the gay spouse, and he often criticizes his wife's sexual needs and desires. In time, this can have a damaging effect

on the wife's self-esteem in the bedroom. Some women are told they are responsible for their husbands' turning to men. This leaves them with a strong sense of sexual inadequacy.

Even though you may be able to intellectually comprehend the situation of marrying a gay man and are dealing with it, emotionally it leaves its scars. One of those scars is usually in the area of sex. If you are having difficulty conquering this problem over a long period of time, it is best to seek counseling with someone who specializes in sexual problems.

Q.   Should I be worried about AIDS?

A.   Most definitely. It never ceases to amaze me that in this day and age of constant reminders and death tolls, men are still not responsible when it comes to having sex with male partners and then with their wives. Through the years, I have counseled dozens of women who contracted AIDS through their husbands and who eventually died a terrible, painful death. For a number of years in the 1980s when AIDS was an automatic death sentence, there seemed to be less risks taken by gay males. But over the last few years, with the discovery of various life-sustaining drugs, it appears that men are taking chances again because they are under the impression that they can continue to live with medication. I have gay friends who have revealed that they are less careful today than five or ten years ago. The truth is that AIDS is *not* a curable disease and people still die from it. If you have the slightest suspicion that your husband has engaged in homosexual activities, even if he staunchly denies it, be safe and take an HIV test. If there is any doubt in your mind about your husband's sexual orientation, make sure that you use protection if you are continuing to have sexual relations with him.

My saddest experiences as a counselor came about over the years were when women would call me to tell me that their husbands had AIDS, that they were dying from AIDS, and now their children were being left as orphans. Early detection of HIV can definitely prolong your life. Ignoring the possibility can result in your untimely death.

Chapter 3

The Gay Husband Checklist

The most frequently asked question from women is if there is any way to detect whether or not their husband is gay and what are the signs.

Unfortunately, there are no definite ways to tell if a man is gay unless he is either honest with you or you catch him in the act. However, there are certain behavior patterns to watch for that may help you make this determination.

First, learn to understand homosexuality. Most people are under the misconception that a man who is gay is effeminate and swishy, as is stereotyped in the mass media. Although this is true of some gay men, it certainly is not representative of most gay men, *especially those who marry!* For instance, my lack of understanding this aspect of homosexuality put my mind at rest about my ex-husband, even when others confronted me with their suspicions. He was an excellent athlete, which certainly exemplifies "machoness" at its best; therefore, how could he possibly be gay?

Sexual activity is another area that is often a giveaway. Although some gay men can certainly sexually perform with females, they are usually not overanxious about doing it.

Touching a woman's vaginal area turns them off. Performing oral sex on their wives is usually out of the question, while wanting it performed on them is a preference.

I have spoken to women who have asked me about behavior patterns that I find to be cause for alarm. This is my checklist:

1. *NORMAL SEXUAL APPETITE*

    If your sexual needs fall into the realm of "normal" without excessiveness and your husband tries to make you think that you are a nymphomaniac, you could have a problem. To a gay man, normal sexual practices are definitely excessive. In my marriage, which was typical of others in this situation, my husband demeaned me for being "too pushy or too aggressive" by wanting to make love with him. I didn't have excessive sexual needs, but rather I had the normal needs of most women. I would have been happy to have sexual relations twice a week during the first few years of my marriage, but that was too much for my husband. After our first year of marriage, he performed once a month for my benefit and it was very empty sex. As much as he pretended to enjoy being with me, I knew that he didn't.

    This made me feel as if I wasn't a worthy lover and took the joy out of it for me as well. No woman wants to feel that she cannot please or satisfy her husband. It makes you feel inadequate and flows over to other parts of your life. And no woman wants to feel as if her husband is doing her a favor by making love to her. It is humiliating and embarrassing.

2. DECLINE IN SEXUAL ACTIVITY EARLY IN THE MARRIAGE

If you experience a spiraling decline in sexual activity within the first few years together, this is a warning sign. All marriages have their peaks and valleys when it comes to sex. This can be caused for a variety of reasons such as financial hardship, family conflicts, emotional traumas, and stress-related problems. However, once the problems are resolved, the sexual activity resumes. Sex for straight men is a common, normal practice satisfying a physical need. Even if the romance and passion has disappeared from the marriage, the need for sexual release is still there. In straight/gay marriages, the decline continues regardless of the circumstances—good or bad! This is because the husband's need for sex is not with a woman, but rather with a man.

The sexual relationship is usually abnormal from the beginning of the relationship in the sense that the frequency is not nearly as high as a heterosexual relationship. But the gay male will try harder in the beginning due to the fear of the female questioning his sexuality. I remember on our honeymoon how Michael insisted that we have sex each day, which was out of character with our usual twice a week at that point. He stated that he wanted me to always remember how wonderful our honeymoon was. He used this as a weapon against me in future arguments to convince me that he was perfectly "normal" sexually—after all, we made love every day on our honeymoon. This was his way of letting me know that if there were sexual problems in the marriage, they were due to my inadequacies, not his.

3.   LACK OF SEXUAL AGGRESSIVENESS BY THE HUS-BAND

In a straight/gay relationship, the woman often finds herself the more sexually aggressive partner. This happens because the gay spouse is not interested in having sex. If left up to him, sex is only performed as often as necessary to keep the premise going that he is "normal." This is not to say that a gay man cannot be satisfied or achieve an orgasm from sex with his straight partner; however, it is not his preference. Clearly, whatever satisfaction a gay man achieves sexually is based on his emotional needs, not his sexual ones.

In all fairness, the majority of gay men love their wives at the time of marriage and are trying their best to make it work. They want to be good husbands and understand that sex is part of the package. They do everything possible to fulfill that part of the marriage, even in a minimal way. But don't underestimate their trying. What may seem like a mediocre to poor performance to a woman is truly a very concerted effort on the part of the gay man.

The best way a woman can understand this is to try to picture herself in a sexual situation with a man who is her best friend but who has absolutely no physical appeal to her. She really loves the man as a friend, and she may even feel he is attractive, but the chemistry is missing. No doubt, if she had to, she could go through the motions and have a sexual encounter. But how often could she continue doing this, even if she loves the person? How rewarding or fulfilling would she find it if she continued doing this just to make the other person happy?

People argue that numerous heterosexual couples find themselves in the same position after a period of time. When the passion and excitement fade due to monotony, growing apart, financial pressures, or other reasons, the thrill is gone and it's difficult, if not impossible, to get those feelings back. But with straight/gay couples, the passion and excitement was never really there, making the woman feel that there is something wrong with her from the beginning. Things only go from bad to worse, never having the chance to experience the wonders of mutually satisfying passion and lovemaking.

4.   *DISGUST OVER NORMAL SEXUAL FUNCTIONS*
    If your husband is turned off by the thought of touching your vaginal area or performing oral sex with you, this could be a sign of a problem. It is not uncommon for a gay man to justify his repulsion of performing perfectly normal heterosexual sex by bragging that all the other women he has been with have never complained about his ability as a lover. This is because he has never had a female partner or certainly limited heterosexual experiences. Clearly, there are straight men who are not interested in performing oral sex with women just as there are straight women who refuse to perform oral sex with men. However, touching a woman's vaginal area does not repulse straight men. Also, straight men are turned on by a woman having an orgasm and will try their best to make this happen. A gay man does not become more sexually aroused by a woman being pleased; therefore, a woman's pleasure is not that important to him.

5. GAY FRIENDS

If your mate's closest friend(s) is gay, this indicates a problem. The gay world is entirely different than the straight one, and even though straight people do have gay friends, it is rare for a straight man to have a close friendship with a gay man. If there is more than one close gay friend, you should be concerned. Some straight men have a gay friend because they grew up with the person or they have are co-workers with a gay male, but that is usually the limit. Most straight men feel threatened by the companionship of a gay male friend and worry whether he will make sexual advances. I would like to say that these fears are unfounded, but in some cases that fear does become a reality.

6.   GAY BARS

A straight man who hangs out in gay bars is definitely suspect. A straight man may visit a gay bar once with a group of friends as a curiosity seeker, but not after that. Straight men are open targets for propositions by gay men for sexual encounters, and this makes them feel extremely uncomfortable. In a gay bar, men are often uninhibited with their sexual gestures. You commonly see men hugging, embracing, kissing, feeling, grinding each other and more because they are in a non-threatening environment where they can be themselves. A straight man is repulsed by a gay bar because of the openness of male sexuality.

7.   GAY PORNO MOVIES

If your husband enjoys going to gay porno movies or watches them at home, you have reason to be concerned. If there is one scene out of many, fine, but if the movies are geared in this direction, watch out! Straight men are not stimulated by gay male sex. Two females having sexual activity or even two males having sexual activity with one female may arouse them. But two men—no way!

8. *HOMOPHOBIC COMMENTS*

If you find your husband out of proportion comments about gay people, gay bars, gay sex, etc., even in a critical way, you may have a problem. Gay men in hiding will often mock and imitate other gay men to throw you off guard and to take deflect your suspicions. Some gay men are self-hating and/or homophobic and will criticize homosexuals because they can't come to terms with their own homosexuality.

9. *EGO BUILDING BY GAY MEN*

If your husband brags about gay men complimenting him on his looks or body and finds it flattering, this is a problem. Straight men are not flattered when other men compliment them. Also, where is he hanging out that often to have more than one gay man compliment him?

One or more of these categories should at least alert you to the fact that there may be a problem. The most important factor in any relationship is the amount of time that you have to get to know a person. You are more likely to discover someone's habits a year or two into the relationship than in the beginning, when it is easy to impress and mislead someone who has stars in her eyes. If you have any cause for suspicion, hold off from making long-term commitments or getting further involved if you are already committed. For instance, if you are planning on children but have any doubts, hold off. Or, if you are supposed to relocate to a new city, delay the move. A gay husband may want his wife to move to a new area away from her family and friends. This takes the wife away from her support system and isolates her, making her more dependent on her spouse.

Chapter 4

The Checklist for Women Who Attract Gay Men

Women also ask me if there is a prototype that a gay man will look for as his wife. Is there a conscious effort on the part of the gay man to find a specific type of woman that would make an ideal spouse?

These are some of the common characteristics I have found in women who marry gay men:

1. LOW SELF-ESTEEM.

Women who have low self-esteem are easy targets for gay men. Women who have low self-esteem are prey for a variety of undesirable men including those who practice physical, mental, and verbal abuse. And, in a society that rewards people for beauty, business savvy, and intelligence, I would estimate that half of all women find themselves lacking in the department of self-esteem for one reason or another. It's not our fault, but rather the fault of a male-driven society that sets these standards of desirability for women. Even if we spend years achieving extraordinary accomplishments, it can take just one jerk to knock down whatever confidence we have built up.

I used to believe that only women who weren't attractive by men's standards of beauty felt bad about themselves. But I learned over the years that even the most beautiful women can lack feelings of self-worth for other reasons too numerous to discuss here. In my support group, I was amazed by some of women who were very attractive. They didn't lack in their social lives, but they ended up with gay husbands anyway.

The women I counseled who maintained a higher self-image walked away from these marriages more quickly because they believed they deserved better. The ones with lower self-esteem prior to marriage tried to make them work in every possible way, fearing loneliness and financial disaster. They believed that a husband, even a gay one, is better than no husband.

Women with low self-esteem equate being alone as being a failure. They are willing to suffer more than other women. A straight/gay marriage robs them of their self-worth, and they often feel as if they are unable to cope alone. The longer they remain in the marriage, the more their self-confidence erodes, regardless of how strong it starts out.

Gay men easily recognize this trait in women. Either consciously or unconsciously, they choose them as wives knowing that they can do what they want without fearing a penalty if they are caught. They have faith that their spouse will accept their homosexuality, and they are often correct.

2.   *LIMITED SEXUAL EXPERIENCES.*

If a woman has had a diversified sex life, she is able to tell more easily when there is something wrong sexually in a relationship. She may not realize it's because her lover is gay, but she will know that something is off. Many of the women that I spoke to over the years had either very limited numbers of lovers or no sexual encounters prior to marriage. A gay man knows that he will have a difficult time having heterosexual sex and therefore tries to find a woman who will not be able to compare.

3.   ABUSIVE SEXUAL EXPERIENCES.

I have spoken to dozens of women who had abusive sexual relationships in the past and were happy to meet someone who was not looking to create a strong sexual relationship. One of my clients, Marybeth, had been raped repeatedly by her stepfather throughout her adolescence. She dreaded having sex with men because of these terrifying experiences. When Marybeth went to college, she took a psychology course and wrote a term paper on incest. A male classmate, Jules, became aware of Marybeth's topic and immediately gravitated to her. He expressed sincere interest and deep compassion about the topic, sensing that she had been an incest victim. He was gay and assumed that she had sexual hang-ups due to her earlier experiences. He admitted to me that she seemed like the perfect choice for a relationship. They had a tremendous amount of things in common, including their jobs, school, and leisure activities. Neither one of them was interested in a sexual relationship. Marybeth did not think that Jules was gay, but rather a wonderful man who appreciated her for who she was—not for what she would put out in the bedroom.

Jules did not reveal his homosexuality to Marybeth during their two-year courtship. They shared moments of intimacy by lying in bed together and holding each other. Jules was fighting his homosexuality and hoping that the right woman would take away his attraction to men. He had two previous relationships with men that had left him feeling "dirty." He suppressed his sexual needs throughout the courtship with Marybeth by resorting to masturbation when he had the need. He told Marybeth that he believed that couples should wait to have sex until they were married, and she was flattered and accepted this explanation.

When they did get married, Jules admitted that he was having some concerns about what would happen next sexually. He loved Marybeth very much, but had trouble having or keeping an erection with her. On their honeymoon, he attempted to perform intercourse, but he was just not capable. Marybeth was not disappointed because she was still overshadowed by her previous abuse problem. She was content with the holding and fondling that both of them were able to do. Ironically, Jules revealed to Marybeth that an uncle had sexually abused him while he was growing up. She transposed her own horrors to him and assumed that was why he had sexual trouble.

Sex never became a major issue to either one during their first year of marriage. They looked for ways to fulfill whatever sexual needs they had, including fondling and touching each other until they reached an orgasm. Jules always felt guilty that he was not able to sexually penetrate Marybeth, but she was still so mentally broken down from her repeated raping that she didn't care. She could have lived this way indefinitely, but Jules couldn't.

One day, he met Carl at work, and there was an instant mutual physical attraction. Jules always wore his wedding band to serve as a deterrent to anyone who might have a physical interest in him. Carl ignored the ring. When Carl would make sexual innuendoes in conversation, Jules laughed them off at first. After a few months, he wasn't laughing anymore. Carl knew Jules was gay from the first day they met. It was a gut feeling—there were no "tell-tale" signs. Maybe it was a glance that lasted too long, or the overly close friendship that developed. By the time Jules and Marybeth celebrated their first wedding anniversary, Jules was sexually involved with Carl.

At first Marybeth didn't know. Jules started to bring Carl home for dinner or to hang out, and Marybeth enjoyed his company. She was glad that Jules had a friend because he didn't have a life outside of her. The trio would go shopping, watch movies, and roam the flea markets together. Carl genuinely liked Marybeth and enjoyed her company. The fact that he was having sex with her husband did not faze him at all.

Marybeth even tried to match Carl up with women, including her younger sister. Carl was not about to reveal his secret to Marybeth and ruin the relationship.

As time went on, Marybeth noticed signs that caused her to think that there might be more than just a friendship between the two men. She quickly dismissed these suspicions, feeling guilty, as if she was betraying Jules. She started observing the interaction between the two men and on a few occasions, noticed little slips. These included too much touching and glances that lasted too long for normal eye contact. Eventually she started to feel like she was the intruder on their relationship. Her observations kicked in too late. By now, Jules was madly in love with Carl, and he was more concerned with Carl's feelings than Marybeth's.

Once Marybeth jokingly made a remark suggesting that something more than friendship was developing between the two men, but Jules reacted with anger. He later admitted that he did that purposely because he wasn't ready to tell the truth. He also knew that Marybeth would feel better if she heard his denials. Even though his wife accepted his sexual limitations, Jules didn't think she would continue to be accepting if she knew he was having relations with someone else.

Jules tried to juggle all ends. Carl was pressuring him to leave Marybeth and move in with him. He tried all kinds of tactics including sex deprivation, talk about his next lover, and even threats to tell Marybeth the truth.

While all of this was going on, Jules was miserable and taking it out on Marybeth. He loved her more than anyone he had loved in his life, but he wasn't in love with her and never could be. He didn't have the same feelings of excitement and passion that he felt for Carl. Jules didn't want to hurt Marybeth, but he was unhappy and blaming her for his unhappiness.

Marybeth knew something was wrong when Carl suddenly stopped coming around. Jules covered up by saying that Carl was busy with a new love interest, but Marybeth didn't understand why they weren't a foursome. Why wouldn't Carl introduce his best friends to his new girlfriend? Jules never responded, but rather changed the subject.

Finally, Jules was on the verge of a nervous breakdown. He felt ripped in half and could no longer cope with his personal agony. He went to Marybeth and held her while he cried hysterically. He begged for her understanding and forgiveness because he could no longer live with the deceit. He blurted out that he and Carl were in a relationship for over a year. He continued that Marybeth was his life, but Carl was his heart. He had to accept that he was gay and didn't want to keep living a lie with someone he loved so much. He explained his doubts about his sexuality since childhood, but hoped that marriage would make the attraction to men disappear. He prayed that his love for Marybeth would take away his gay desires.

They both cried and Marybeth felt totally numb. On one level she was not surprised or shocked. This was her first relationship and she didn't know what to expect. She believed that Jules was her male counterpart. Since she was complacent with limited sexual activity, there was nothing odd about another incest survivor being complacent. Homosexuality never crossed her mind until the friendship with Carl.

Postscript—Marybeth told Jules that she could accept his homosexuality as long as she didn't see him with a lover. Jules was overwhelmed by her generosity. Carl wasn't. He wanted a total relationship and forced Jules to choose. Jules left Marybeth and moved in with Carl.

Eventually Marybeth worked with a therapist who specialized in incest victims and was able to move past her sexual fears. She met a wonderful man and remarried. Today she has two children and a loving relationship with her husband. Jules died in 1993 from AIDS. Carl was not infected with the virus and stayed loyally by his side until his death. Jules and Carl had a turbulent relationship, which was not monogamous; however, they remained living together. At the funeral, Marybeth and Carl made their peace.

4.   *TOLERANCE AND ACCEPTANCE.*

Some wives of gay men are the most tolerant and accepting people that I have ever known. They would be my choice as friends because they have a great sense of humanity. A gay man is attracted to this type of woman because he believes that if the news should come out, the wife will accept the situation because she is so accepting of people in general. These women are different than the ones with low self-esteem. They are generous in their compassion for their gay husbands in the quest for coming to terms with homosexuality, but they cannot accept a gay husband. These women have an easier time leaving than the wives who have low self-esteem.

5.   *UNINFORMED WOMEN.*

Ignorance is the best line of strategy for a gay man who wants a wife. I have spoken to hundreds of women throughout middle America who couldn't understand the concept of having a gay husband. Living in a big city where there is a large gay population is quite different than in a small town where the entire population wouldn't be enough to fill a gay bar. Gay communities, gay bars, and gay organizations don't exist in these towns. Anyone openly gay would be subjected to physical violence and ridicule.

Discovering your husband is gay is a shock to women who live in large cosmopolitan areas where people have been exposed to homosexuality. Imagine how much more disturbing it is for women from small towns who have no understanding because they have never knowingly met anyone who is gay.

A gay man can easily hide his sexuality from a woman living under these circumstances.

6. *WOMEN SEEKING GAY HUSBANDS.*

Lest anyone should misunderstand this concept, let me be very clear. A minute percentage of women are aware that their husbands are gay at the time of the marriage. I find it difficult to believe that any woman would knowingly marry a gay man, but it does happen. From the small number of women I counseled who did, I cannot come up with a generalized profile because each one's reasons are different. The saddest story I heard was from a woman who attended one of our support meetings.

Catherine, 26, was a large-boned, overweight female with mousy brown hair hanging over her face, skin scarred from acne, and chipped teeth. She brought Brett, her husband of two years, to the meeting. Brett was a double for Brad Pitt. He had a blonde hair, blue eyes, perfect white teeth, and an athletic body. I felt uncomfortable on the night of their visit because the other gay husbands attending the meeting were making passes at him. We had set the ground rules at our first meeting that there was to be no interaction between husbands who were part of the group. I suppose I was naïve, but I had faith in the gay men in our group.

Catherine met Brett at a gay bar. She admitted that she was "fag hag," a gay terminology for a straight female who hangs out in gay bars. She started visiting the gay bars in her early 20's when a gay male friend invited her to join him for a drink. She immediately felt comfortable unlike the straight bars where she was always a wallflower. The only time a man ever spoke to her in a straight bar was when he was drunk, and it was never an enticing conversation. She enjoyed the company of the gay men who treated her like a sister and routinely went to the bars two or three times a week. he night Brett walked in a bar, her heart skipped a beat and there was love in her eyes. She (as well as most of the men in the bar) wanted him. Catherine knew that dating a gay man was not the same as having gay friends, but didn't care. She walked over to Brett and started talking, and the two became fast friends. After a few weeks, Catherine revealed her feelings to Brett. She was in love with him and wanted to be part of his life under any terms. She could accept his lifestyle if he was willing to be in a relationship with her.

Brett cared about Catherine, but his feelings for her were different than her feelings for him. He would never love her in the same way a straight man would love her. But Catherine had never been loved by a straight man so this was a moot point. They went out three or four times a week and grew closer the first year. Brett saw beauty within Catherine that no one else had bothered to look for. He was the first and only man who ever took the time to know her as a person. Catherine was obsessively devoted to Brett. She overpowered him with a pure love that he had not found in any male relationship.

After a year, Catherine asked Brett to marry her. She understood that Brett would be dating men and making love to them, and she could accept this as long as he would come home to her. Through the first year of their friendship, Brett was open with Catherine about the men he was seeing and even introduced her to them. Catherine was always cordial, but inside she was hurting. She believed that if they married, someday Brett would give up the gay lifestyle and learn to love her the same way that she loved him. Until that time, she would suffer in silence.

Brett thought it would be "neat" to have a wife and live a gay lifestyle. To him, gay was primarily a sexual state of mind. He hadn't met a man who offered him the family life that Catherine proposed. And Catherine was the best—she knew about his gay sexual relations but never interfered or questioned him. She filled the other voids in his life, so why not have the best of both worlds? He agreed to marry her.

The ceremony took place at the gay bar where they met and all of their friends attended. By that time, Catherine's only friends were the men from the bar. She had no girlfriends and limited contact with her family who lived in the Midwest. When Catherine and Brett came to our meeting, they were looking for acceptance and understanding. They didn't receive it. Our members had difficulty grasping the concept that someone wanted to marry a man knowing up front that he was gay and having sexual relations with other men but not with her. Catherine admitted there was no sex between them, but she retorted that many straight couples stop having sex after a while. Sex was a small part of any relationship—it was the other things that counted.

I think we may have been less judgmental before Catherine made a comment that alienated us. She defensively said, "How would I be able to find such a handsome man who was straight? People look at us wherever we go, and I feel good when other women look at Brett and wish they were me." That said it all for us.

The other women I met who knew about their husbands' homosexuality before marriage had their own set of psychological hang-ups. Some were victims of sexual abuse as children, some had previous physically or emotionally abusive relationships with men, and others were socially unable to connect with straight men. Some of these women never found the companionship with a straight male who cared about them in the way a gay man does on a platonic basis. This led them to falsely hope that their gay friends might change if the circumstances were right. Some believed that they could become personal "messiahs" and rescue these men from an empty life of homosexuality. I was always saddened after meeting these women because I knew that their low self-esteem prior to the marriage would only deteriorate further as the marriage progressed.

7. *WOMEN WITH THEIR OWN SEXUAL IDENTITY PROBLEMS.*

I have met couples who both came to terms with their homosexuality after they married. The first time I met a twosome like this blew my mind. One spouse not knowing was understandable, but both spouses? As I started meeting other couples in this situation, I began to understand how this happens. Sexuality is such a complex situation, and homosexuality complicates things even more.

I had various responses with this combination. Several of the men said they were attracted to their lesbian mates because there was a sense of boyishness or butchness about them that they felt more attracted to than feminine looking women. Others said it was because they were looking for a mate who wasn't sexually aggressive because they were not feeling sexually attracted to women.

Their lesbian mates were also confused about their identities. They were hoping that they could lead a "straight" life even though they had doubts. A man who was not typically macho or sexually aggressive seemed like an ideal candidate. Even though all of the couples I met were aware that something was off about them heterosexually, most had not come to terms with their homosexuality. The majority of the men had experimented sexually with other men before marriage, but did not feel they could fit in the gay world. The majority of women had not experimented with other women prior to marriage, but knew that they had feelings of attraction. All of these couples loved each other on some level prior to marriage, and most of them hoped that marriage would take away their attraction to people of the same sex.

Several of the men admitted they suspected that their wives were lesbians when they met, which was what attracted them to such a relationship. Some of the men were honest about previous homosexual encounters, but added they did not find it fulfilling. This justified their wanting to marry a woman. Several of the wives confided that they felt a sense of relief when they learned this information because they felt their husbands could accept whatever would happen in the future if they actively sought out women.

At least half of these couples had children together. But eventually, the couples that I kept in touch with broke up when they became ready to experience their newly accepted homosexuality. Sometimes it was the man who left, but usually it was the woman when she found the right woman who could offer her what she needed in a relationship. It seemed that women were able to accept their homosexuality easier than the men. Perhaps it's because lesbian women as a rule have more stable relationships than gay men.

Chapter 5

How and Why Women Marry Gay Men

Over the years, people on the sidelines have repeatedly asked me this question: "How could you not have known that your husband was gay?" They claim that either on a conscious or unconscious level, I must have known at some point that my husband was gay. I don't agree with their thinking.

My experiences with gay men were typical of the majority of other straight women's, but probably slightly more extensive. When I went to high school in the 1960s, I wasn't aware that I knew anyone who was gay until years afterwards. Three guys I had relationships with during high school came to me at later periods of my life and admitted to me that they were gay. Some of you might think, "Ah hah! Then there was something that drew you to gay men." But I don't believe this is the case at all, and after I explain, I think that you might not only understand, but also wonder about some of your past relationships with certain men.

First, let's review again what most of us believe to be identifiable traits about gay men. It is our understanding that if a man is gay, he is involved sexually with someone else who is a man. This is what makes a man gay. Most people also are under the misconception that if a man is gay, he has stereotypical characteristics that are identified with gay men such as an effeminate walk, a sing-song talk, the limp wrist, a handshake with no grasp, ultra flamboyant clothes, and endless chit-chat about female-oriented topics.

As I stated earlier, I probably had more exposure to gay men than most people had because I lived in Southern California in the late 1960s, where some people were openly and outwardly gay and proud of it. I remember when I first moved to Santa Monica, California at the age of 17 and I met several gay guys who lived on the beach where I hung out. My friends introduced me to a young man, Glen, who was 20 years old. He was six feet three inches tall with wavy dark blonde, shoulder-length hair. He was not particularly handsome, but he had such a charming and charismatic personality. At the time, Glen was at the end of a two-year relationship with a 19-year-old, Larry, whose name he had tattooed inside a big heart on his arm. Larry, like Glen, seemed obviously gay to me. His mannerisms were very effeminate, from the way he walked, to the way he threw back his long brown hair. Larry was also cute and endearing, crying daily because Glen hurt his feelings. These two were not only my visual perception of typical gays, but they also used the lingo of calling Larry "she" or "her" in their conversations. There was a defined role of male and female that each one played.

Glen also had a 40-year-old sugar daddy, Roger, who appeared to be a typical straight businessman. This was the first exposure

I knowingly had to a gay man who appeared straight. Roger was a quiet, small-framed man of five feet, four inches, with thinning brown hair and blue eyes. He fell in love with Glen three years earlier when they met at a party. Roger agreed to pay Glen's bills and give him spending money in return for having sex once a week. Roger was also allowed to visit Glen one other day of the week in the chaotic apartment that was always filled with people. Roger had to accept the fact that Glen was with other men, and he had no say as to whom Glen was living or sleeping with. Glen always treated Roger in an embarrassing, humiliating way in front of company, including me. I felt sorry for Roger and after a typical tongue-lashing, asked why he stayed with Glen. He always replied that he was in love and couldn't stand to live without him. Yes, it hurt Roger to see Glen lying in bed with Larry or the barrage of guys that came after Larry, but he had to sit in silence and endure the pain—or else Glen said he would end the relationship. It was hard for me to believe that Roger was gay from looking or talking to him. He had an excellent job in real estate. He still lived with his mother and never entertained the thought of dating women. He claimed to be a "confirmed bachelor" to anyone who questioned him.

At 17, this all seemed strange to me. I had heard about homosexuals in books, but I never had "officially" met any. It seemed to me back then that there was a solution for these "poor, misguided homosexuals." There was nothing that the love of a good woman couldn't cure. I was convinced that if Glen found the right woman, he could turn into the right man. And who would be a better "right woman" for him than me? After two months, I found myself falling in love with Glen and tried to convince him to give me a turn in his life. After all, we were excellent friends, and it would only take a few adjustments to move from a friendship into a relationship.

In retrospect, I suppose that Glen felt he owed it to himself to see if he could be straight. He cared greatly for me as a friend, and we entertained the idea of eloping in Mexico. We even attempted to have sexual relations on three different occasions just to say that we could do it. It was actually amusing trying to have sex with a man who could not keep an erection no matter how hard he tried to fantasize me as a man! I think this is what made us realize we could never work as a couple. I admitted defeat—all of my love could not make this man straight. And it also left a deeply embedded brain message that a gay man could not have straight sex with a woman. This meant I didn't need to worry about future men who might be gay—I'd be able to tell immediately when we got into bed. Right? Well, not exactly. I mentioned earlier the three guys I went with in high school came to terms with their homosexuality in later years. Here is the story of each of them and how their news was revealed.

At the age of 15 in 1966, I was an overweight teenager who didn't fit in among the popular and beautiful. This didn't stop me from flirting or trying to find a boyfriend. The older brother of one of my classmates started talking to me at the bus stop each morning, and before we knew it, we became close friends. Andy was a six foot two inch giant next to my five foot one inch frame. I was always attracted to taller men because they seemed to offer a sense of protection and security to me. He had a ruddy complexion from acne scarring, but other than that, he was handsome with dark brown eyes and hair.

By the summer, Andy and I were an item. His family was vacationing for the summer in Atlantic City, New Jersey, a two-hour bus ride from Philadelphia. Each week, I would sneak on a bus, spend the day with Andy on the beach, come home, and try to figure out how to tell my mother how I got so sunburned!

Unlike other boys I dated that year, Andy made no attempt to do anything physical with me other than hold hands and kiss me goodbye. I was so impressed to find someone who liked and respected me for who I was and not for what I was willing to "put out."

Andy's family was wealthy, and they were unhappy with his choice of a girlfriend. They didn't think that I was from the right social strata for their family and convinced Andy to break up with me by the end of the summer. He was mysteriously whisked out of state to military school with no forwarding address and no information from the family. I was not heartbroken because I was so in love with Andy, but rather because my low self-esteem was knocked a notch lower when Andy's sister told me that his family thought I was not good enough for him.

Nine years later, Andy called me from Miami Beach. He had seen me on a nationally televised show and tracked me back to my office in New York. I was shocked and excited to hear from him. We spoke for a half-hour, and he promised to write me a long letter catching up on the last decade, which I received the following week. He apologized for mysteriously disappearing all those years before, but he explained his parents had made his life unbearable over our relationship. They even threatened not to send him to college if he continued to see me, and he gave in to their demands, never feeling good or right about it.

His letter went on to explain that since that time, he had relocated to Miami Beach and there found the lover he had been searching for. The person's name was David, and they had been living together for two years. He said that he came to terms with being homosexual four years earlier after fighting it all his life.

I wrote back to Andy stating how my heart went out to him and how sorry I felt for his being gay. After all, I knew how difficult being gay could be from my earlier California exposures. Andy was very angry over that statement and wrote back, "Don't feel sorry for me, because I don't feel sorry for myself. I am happy in my life and feel content and fulfilled. I am different than other men, but no less happy."

When I visited Andy several months later, he looked more handsome than ever, and there certainly was a happier expression on his face than the one I had last seen when we were together. I also noted that his characteristics were much more effeminate than when I had known him. I thought to myself that if I were to meet him now, I could definitely tell he was gay!

In 11th grade, I was best friends with a guy named Richard. He was a year younger than I was, and we became inseparable after school hours. Richard was popular with his peers, and several girls had mad crushes on him and would come to me for advice on how to win his favor.

We never thought of each other romantically in the beginning; however, as the months passed, we were spending so much time with each other that we started questioning our feelings for each other. We never fell in love or had the kind of painful feelings that young love brings, but we just felt so good being together.

One night when Richard was visiting me, he brought over a bottle of wine and we began drinking. We were feeling the effects of the alcohol and started holding each other on the couch. One thing led to the next, and before long, we were on the floor, attempting to have sex. Although we went through the motions, there was a sense of emptiness about it. We never completed the act, and I think we both realized that a relationship outside of friendship was not in the cards.

Richard and I remained best friends after this incident. Our sexual moment did not put any distance between us at all. One summer night, two years later, Richard and I went to New York and spent the night in a hotel together. We slept in the same bed, but there was no physical contact at all. We were buddies and happy to remain that way.

Shortly after this, I moved to California and the next year, Richard went to college in Boston. We stayed in touch by mail for a while, but as he became more acclimated to his new environment, his correspondence lessened. I missed him but was busy with my own life and activities. When Richard called me nearly a year later to tell me that he would be in town and wanted to have dinner, I was thrilled for the opportunity to see him and catch up.

We met at our favorite restaurant in Center City, Philadelphia. I had just moved back to Philadelphia from California and rented an apartment in the city, so it was a convenient place for both of us to meet. After the customary hugs, kisses, and excitement, we sat down and ordered dinner. While waiting for our food, I chattered on about my life events since our last time together, never thinking that Richard was building up the courage to tell me his news. When I ran out of breath and asked him to tell me everything going on in his life, there was suddenly a strange silence. When I questioned him what was wrong, he said, "There is no easy way to say this, so

I'll just say it—I'm gay." Having just returned from California, I didn't seem to be too shocked.

Richard went on to explain that he suspected that he was gay for a number of years, but he couldn't come to terms with it. During our high school days we had a friend named Joey who everyone assumed was gay because he displayed the stereotypical mannerisms of homosexuality. Richard was so different in his gestures and behavior from Joey that he was sure that he couldn't be the same. Besides, he was adored by so many popular girls in school who wanted to go out with him. He dated a dozen of those girls during high school for different periods of time, and although there were no real commitments, he did seem to have his fair share of fun.

Richard's attraction to men increased during his high school senior year, but he refused to give in to these feelings because he was scared to face the inevitable. He remarked about our weekend trip to New York the summer before he graduated high school. He remembered my remarks about men we passed on the streets whom I found attractive. While I assumed Richard was looking at women, he was really looking at the same men I admired wondering if we had the same taste. He still had not acted on his feelings, but once he started college, that changed.

There was a gay and lesbian support group on campus, and shortly after his arrival, he went there for information. After that, he spent his freshman year exploring his homosexuality and finally came to accept himself for what he was. Ironically, Richard's mannerisms, like Andy's, had changed. I'm not sure whether these mannerisms were purposely hidden or if being with other gay people made them surface. Richard said he finally felt at peace, and although his parents weren't happy about his new lifestyle, they didn't cut him off. In fact, they had allowed him to bring home one of his lovers during a semester break. I think that it was easier for his parents to deal with his homosexuality than what happened to him later in his life.

I will tell the story of our future meetings because it teaches an important lesson about homosexuality to those people who still believe that people have a choice in their sexuality. Sadly, the overwhelming majority of straight people I talk to today, with all of the information that is available, still believe that sexuality is a choice.

Richard and I lost track of each other after that year. Our lives were both going down different roads, and due to the distance between us, we lost touch. Our paths crossed again eight years later when I lived in New York. I was walking in midtown Manhattan to Macy's department store when a man passed me in the opposite direction. We saw each other, but it took us ten seconds to realize the connection. At the same moment, we turned around and ran to each other, simultaneously hugging and crying. After all of our years apart, it was such a shock finding each other in downtown New York.

I begged Richard to have a cup of coffee with me, but he seemed uncomfortable with the idea. I couldn't understand his hesitancy and asked him what was wrong. He told me that he had been following my political career, and based on what he had seen, didn't think I would be very understanding about his current activities. I couldn't imagine what they could be. After all, I had no problem dealing with his homosexuality. We had established that years ago. What else could he be referring to? He didn't want to discuss it, but a light went off in my head. He was walking towards the New Yorker Hotel down the block from

Macy's, which was occupied by the followers of Reverend Moon. Throughout the mid and late 1970s, Reverend Moon led the largest cult movement in the country. Thousands of young people from middle and upper class families were selling flowers in airports, train stations, and on the streets to raise the millions of dollars that it took to keep the cult leader living in an elite style. I had met several of these mindless followers who had been alienated from their families and given up their lives to lead the exhausting merry-go-round kind of cult life that Reverend Moon subjected them to. I came out and asked him, "Are you a Moonie?" Richard replied, "Yes."

He went on to explain that he was one of Moon's public relations representatives. The group was publishing a daily national newspaper and Richard was the editor. He also told me that he was getting married the following month in a group wedding with hundreds of other people. I asked how that was possible since he was gay, but he informed me that Reverend Moon had "cured" his homosexuality. Now he was about to embark on a new life with a new wife from Korea that he would meet on his wedding day.

I guess I was still naïve because even at that point of time I thought that gay people could change—or at least some gay people could change. My proof why I thought this change was possible for some gay people will be told shortly after this story.

I saw Richard two more times after that chance meeting. His cult leaders told him he was not allowed to socialize with me, giving him no choice. All of my attempts to contact him were denied by the switchboard operators at the New Yorker Hotel.

The years passed and I rarely thought about Richard until I saw him on an ABC 20/20 news documentary in 1993. The previews of the program earlier in the week kept advertising life studies of homosexuals who had been "cured." Naturally, I was very interested in seeing this program because by then I knew that there is no "cure" for changing sexuality. In the years after my marriage, I continually read articles about gays who were "cured," circulated by religious organizations who condemned homosexuality. There was publicity about religious groups who ran sessions for gays using aversion therapy in the form of electrical shocks while watching homosexuals together to encourage them not to act on these impulses. These success stories were always being touted for the non-believers like me.

The star of the 20/20 show turned out to be none other than my friend Richard. He was shown with his Korean wife and two young children in a loving family portrait of a happy family. Richard told the story about his homosexual experiences during his late teens and early twenties. He stated that he went for help, without mentioning the source of the help, and, as a result, he was now "cured and straight." His proof was his wife and children. His story went on for about fifteen minutes and never once mentioned Reverend Moon or his arranged marriage. It infuriated me that millions of Americans were only being given part of a story and not the part that was important. When someone's mind is controlled by outside forces, he can be talked into believing anything, including a change in his sexuality. This kind of story does more harm to gay people than a mob of homophobic crazies because it fuels the minds of sensible, rational people to start thinking like that mob of crazies. It also makes gay people question their own sexuality and sanity while it gives false hopes to those who are looking for a miracle.

The mind is a fragile machine. There are many educated lost souls in this world who are looking for a leader to tell them what to do rather than to trust their own judgment. Even in the 1990s, we have seen examples of cult movements where highly educated people have committed group suicide because they were convinced that their leaders were divine and ordered them to die. I believe this happens more frequently when people are self-hating about what they are. Therefore, I would not be surprised at all to find an out-of-proportion percentage of cult members comprised of people who are confused about their sexuality.

We still live in a society that emphatically tells us that homosexuality is wrong. Gay people are criticized, ridiculed, and often cut off from families and friends. The message is that homosexuality is a choice that people consciously make. Someone who can perform heterosexual sex even if it is not desirable or preferable is compelled to give the "straight life" a chance because in all other respects it is easier.

Richard was such a fun-loving, outwardly happy teenager. When I saw him as an adult under the influence, he was a totally changed person filled with reserve and seriousness. My best friend had disappeared into the will of a stranger who controlled his life.

My third story begins at the end of my junior year of high school. I started dating a young man, Derrick. We met in one of our classes, and from the moment I saw him early in the semester, I couldn't take my eyes off him. He was one of the most handsome guys I had ever seen, standing six feet tall with dark brown hair and eyes. His good looks made him the talk of the girls in school.

He often said hello to me through that year, and on our last day of class, I had the courage to give him my phone number and invite him to get together during the summer if he was available. I never dreamt he would call me, but he did several weeks into June.

Derrick invited me to dinner and I suspected it was because he had an agenda other than dinner. On our first date, we went for Chinese food in a neighborhood restaurant. Afterwards, we went driving in his car and eventually, we ended up at a big make-out place. I waited for his sexual advances to begin, but it didn't happen. We spent the next two hours casually talking and then he took me home. He walked me to the door and gave me an unpassionate goodnight kiss on the lips. I doubted that I would ever hear from him again, but surprisingly, he called several days later and asked me out.

Over the next few dates, I kept waiting to find us sexually entangled, but it didn't happen. Derrick claimed that he found me interesting and fun to be with, and I was under the definite impression he wanted more than friendship. We started talking daily, and he invited me to his home for dinner once a week. I met his parents who were wealthy professionals, and they seemed not to approve of me, much like Andy's parents, but didn't interfere.

After six weeks of steady dating, we finally moved beyond holding hands and kissing. By the end of the summer, we were having sexual relations. It didn't happen every time we were together, but usually once a week. Although I had previous relationships with guys, I was too young and too sexually immature at that age to understand the difference between good and bad sex. I knew we had a problem, but I could never pinpoint it.

Derrick was moody and sullen at times, which played greatly into my insecurities. I still didn't understand why he was dating me when he could have been dating the most beautiful and popular girls in school. Whenever Derrick went into one of his quiet moods, I was sure he was getting ready to break up with me no matter how he assured me that it wasn't my fault.

After nine months of steady dating, I broke up with Derrick because I could not deal with his feelings of negativity during his frequent mood swings. Shortly after that, I moved to California and our lives moved in different directions.

I called Derrick four years later after the break-up of a two-year live-in relationship. I was feeling depressed about my life and thought perhaps I could recreate a time that seemed happier to me. It's funny how human it is to fantasize a mediocre relationship into a good one when a worse one comes along!

By this time, Derrick had just started medical school and invited me to spend the weekend with him in upstate Pennsylvania. Once there, it seemed as if nothing had changed from several years before—especially in bed. Yes, we had sex, but it seemed very empty and unfulfilling. By now, I had experienced good sex and knew the difference. But okay, I knew sometimes sex could improve over time. Both of us seemed willing to recreate our relationship from high school, but it seemed so forced and difficult. After a few months, we just stopped talking to each other and knew that it was over.

Our paths crossed six years later after the break-up of my first marriage. Once again, I thought it was worth a try and tracked Derrick down to his new home in Massachusetts. He seemed surprised to hear from me after so much time. I knew from his parents that he was still single, and I thought perhaps this was the right time for us to try again. I was then living in New York and gave him my phone number, encouraging him to call me when he came into town.

That call came six months later at a time when we were both without partners. When Derrick walked into my office, I was thrown off guard. Only six years had passed since our last visit, but he looked like a totally different man. His dress was rather disheveled, he had gained at least thirty pounds, and a portion of his upper hair had fallen out while the remainder looked unkempt. He had never fully recovered from a bout with Bell's Palsy which left one side of his mouth lopsided when he spoke and smiled. I tried to cover my disappointment, but it was difficult. Whatever physical attraction I once had for Derrick was gone. I wondered if I could recapture the feelings of excitement that I once had as a love-struck teenager.

Derrick took me to dinner in a quiet French restaurant, and then we went back to my apartment where we enjoyed a bottle of wine. We talked through most of the night and he told me about his life since our last time together.

Derrick became employed as an oncologist in a Massachusetts hospital two years earlier when he was awarded a fellowship. He bought a single home overlooking a lake, which gave him the peace and solitude he needed in his life. He had met numerous women over the years, especially nurses in the hospitals. He had serious relationships with two of those nurses, but they didn't work out. During that conversation, Derrick also mentioned that he had been involved with two men for a short time, but afterwards decided that he was not interested in men. He explained that it was normal for most men to experiment sometime in their lives, and he had done just that.

I was still somewhat naïve about men having these kinds of experiences, but Derrick made it sound so natural that I accepted that he experimented twice and realized that he was straight. He gave no indication that he had any further interest in men, but rather stated that it wasn't his "thing."

Our night ended with sex as if we needed to rekindle whatever remnants of the past were left. Once again, it wasn't great. We kissed goodbye with promises to talk and get together soon. After the next few conversations, we decided to give our relationship one more try. Derrick always kidded that we were like Barbara Streisand and Robert Redford in the movie, The Way We Were, about two college sweethearts that meet up years later and try to rekindle a relationship that never worked to start with.

We met at least two or three times each month. Either Derrick would drive to New York or I would fly to Massachusetts to spend long weekends together. This went on for six months, but once again, old patterns returned and my old insecurities resurfaced. I needed verbal reassurance that I was loved and Derrick was short on words. They were difficult for him to express, and I felt as if I was always seeking his approval. Even though I had come a long way in my life, I still did not feel worthy of this brilliant man who could have his choice of women but chose to be with me.

Our sex life was out of synch. This is the only way I can describe it. Derrick was going through the motions but something was missing. There was no intimacy prior to or following our lovemaking. It was mechanical. I really didn't enjoy it but hoped in time it would improve. He lacked the sense of passion and romance important to me throughout my life.

We were in the planning stages of moving in together when I met Michael, who swept me off my feet. He was fast to fill the void that was missing in my relationship with Derrick. Where Derrick was cold and detached, Michael was warm and expressive. He was quick to express his feelings of love days into the relationship, which was something that Derrick was never able to do.

Derrick tracked me down after two weeks of avoiding communication other than his talking to my answering machine. It was very difficult breaking the news to him that I had met someone else. He couldn't understand how two weeks earlier we were making the same plans to move in together which were now canceled out by a stranger I had just met.

It was difficult explaining this to Derrick, and I admitted that I wasn't sure if I was making the right decision. But I also resolved that moving in with him would not have been the right thing either. I felt I had to give my impulsive heart a chance, and I apologized for hurting him once again.

I kept in touch with Derrick after I married Michael. He wasn't exactly sure why I kept calling him, and I didn't know myself. I suppose I knew from the beginning that I had made a bad decision when I married Michael and wasn't ready to completely let go of the past. A year after I married Michael, Derrick decided to move to New York because he had a prestigious job offer in a local hospital. I helped him find an apartment several blocks away from where I lived. In spite of the close proximity, Derrick made it clear that we were not going to be close friends—just casual acquaintances when I needed to talk to him. One time when Michael was feeling very ill, I called Derrick for help and he came over. That was the only time Derrick and Michael met, and it was awkward for the three of us.

The following year Derrick transferred to a hospital in Washington, D.C. I told him I would keep in touch and followed up on that promise every six months. Our conversations were usually strained and short, but I felt compelled to keep in touch with him.

In 1987, several years after my marriage ended and my support group dissolved, I called Derrick for my biyearly chat. A man answered the phone and told me that Derrick was not home. I asked whom I was talking to, and he stated that he was Derrick's roommate. For the first time, this eerie feeling came over me. When Derrick returned my call, I came right out and asked him if he was gay. He replied, "Yes. How did you know?" By that time, I was so aware of all of the signs that it was obvious to me. Everything finally started to make sense. I now understood why things never totally meshed in our relationship. That conversation was our last conversation.

Some friends advised me not to write this chapter, lest people should think that I am drawn to gay men and have created these tragic situations on my own. I know this is not the case at all. First, let's look at the traits that all of these men had in common to determine if I on some conscious or unconscious level could have known that these men were gay.

All of the men in question, Andy, Richard, Derrick, and Michael, were very handsome men. With the exception of Derrick, they all had outgoing and friendly personalities. They seemed nurturing, supporting, and respectful of me. None of them seemed to be looking at me as a sex object, which was what most women hope for in their lives. They were all sought after by pretty and popular females. Most importantly, why would I think they were gay?

In the cases of Derrick and Michael, both of them performed in bed and reached an orgasm. As I mentioned, it wasn't great sex, but I had worse sex with several other men. In retrospect, they were probably gay, too! I say that now because I have experienced wonderful sexual relationships with straight men, and I know that there is a difference in the way that straight men feel and respond to sex. You can tell that they totally enjoy making love with a woman and want to do anything that will enhance the sexual experience. Now in my forties, I have been most fortunate to find the ultimate love of my life who for over six years has made every sexual experience exciting and fulfilling.

Of the thousands of women I have worked with, a handful claimed that they had sexually satisfying relationships with their gay husbands on a regular basis. These are exceptions to the rule. The rest of the women never had a sexually satisfying relationship or much of a sexual relationship at all. To the credit of some of the gay husbands, they tried their best. They really wanted to satisfy their wives,because in most cases, they loved them on some level. But it is impossible to keep living a lie forever, and thus, the sexual part of the relationship deteriorates within a short period of time.

Chapter 6

SOGA—Spouses of Gays Association

Following the end of my marriage, I was desperate to learn more about women who were or had been in my situation. I felt isolated and alone. I was left to struggle as a single parent with two young babies while dealing with a lot of emotional issues. When Michael left in 1982, I felt it was a stigma to have a gay husband. I was afraid to tell people lest they judge me. I feared that they would look at the failure of my marriage as my failure. After all, how could I marry a man who was gay? And if I didn't know he was gay, maybe he wasn't. Maybe I turned him gay. Michael certainly accused me of that numerous times when I would confront him and ask him if he was "bisexual." I still didn't think in terms of "gay." How could a man be gay and yet still have sex with a woman?

Michael never admitted that he was gay or bisexual during any point in our marriage. However, he had mentioned through periods of frustration in our arguments that, "If I was gay, could you blame me? You're so pushy...demanding...overweight...etc., that you could turn a man turn gay." Not knowing enough about homosexuality, I bought into the accusation. That made me become much more of a silent partner, not wanting to feel as if I had failed my husband as a woman and as a wife. Naturally, that was the beginning of the end of any self-esteem I developed over the years. When your ability as a woman is constantly challenged and denounced, it is impossible not to personalize this and eventually start believing it.

I went to the library in search of literature that would explain this situation, only to come back empty-handed. I scoured the bookstores to find that no one had written any books on this subject. I gave up, believing that I was the only woman who was in the situation.

Almost six months later, I was standing in the checkout line at the supermarket and my eyes were drawn to one of the women's magazines with a headline, "Women Who Are Married To Gay Men." I grabbed the magazine, rushed home, and sat down to read it. Although it only discussed the case histories of two women in depth and the results of four other marriages, I was thrilled to find that I was not the only woman in this situation.

As the article suggested at the end, I looked in my local telephone book in the section with social service organizations. I was shocked to see a listing for "Women Involved with Gays" (WIG) and immediately called the number. A friendly man named Alan answered the phone and told me that he was the head of the organization "Gay Fathers" in Philadelphia. I described my situation and told him that I wanted to get information about the wives' group. He explained that over the years, a number of women had inquired about starting a support group for the wives of their members, but the project never got off the ground. He was willing to supply me with the list of names if I wanted to call them and start a group. I was excited about this undertaking because I was anxious to meet other women who were in this situation in hopes of learning how they were coping. I needed to know how this had happened to me and if other women understood the dynamics better than I did.

I started calling the women on the list one by one. I was discreet because I had no idea whether or not they were still in their marriages or had moved on in their lives. Alan had no indication of how recently these women had inquired about information, and I was cautious when I approached them on the phone. When I called, I introduced myself and told them how I had received their phone number. Almost all of the initial twenty-four women on the list were receptive to my call. I took notes on each person so I could remember her status for the future. Some of them had started new lives and wanted to put this experience behind them. They had no interest in joining a support group or sharing their experiences with others. But twelve women were quite excited about the idea.

I had been an excellent organizer from my earlier years as a political activist. I knew the amount of work that went into starting a new group, and I was willing to devote the time to it. When I found my nucleus of women, I invited them to my home for our initial meeting. Although I was forming the group, I felt that everyone should have input into what we would be doing.

Each one of the new members was living a different story, and each story was intriguing to me. The main couple of the group that would remain a driving force until we disbanded was Cindy and Ray. Cindy was a queen-size, outgoing woman who had been married to Ray for twenty-two years. She hid nothing about their lives together—she was the bluntest woman I had ever met, bordering on vulgarity, but with a comedic wit and bubbling personality that kept everyone laughing at each meeting. Ray was the opposite. He was small and wiry with a sarcastic streak, which he displayed openly in every conversation. He was effeminate and stereotypical of the gay males that I was familiar with. Cindy and Ray were as opposite as two people could be. There was constant friction throughout the years of marriage, but they had raised three children in the midst of their turmoil.

When I met Cindy, she was involved in a relationship with a heterosexual man, and Ray had recently broken up with a homosexual lover. From early in their marriage, they each had separate love lives but also maintained a physical relationship with each other. This was not Ray's choice—but Cindy's insistence. Cindy said that if Ray wanted her for wife, then he would have to perform his "husbandly" duties on her every week like clockwork. She demanded that Ray perform oral sex on her, which he claimed to despise, but he went along with it to keep the peace.

Pamela was the next member of our nucleus. Pamela was an Italian beauty who was also full-sized, like Cindy and me. She was the single mother of two teenage children, a daughter and son. Her husband, Bill, had left the family several years before and moved to Florida. He had never been financially responsible to Pamela or the children throughout their marriage, and now that he moved away, he had minimal contact and sent virtually no child support. Neither Cindy nor Pamela had been aware that their husbands were gay prior to their marriages; however, both husbands had actively been practicing homosexuality without revealing this information to their wives until after the marriages.

Kitty and Paul were also members of our founding team. Their situation was somewhat different than the others. Kitty, a small-framed, pixie-like woman of 30, knew that Paul was gay before she married him. She fell in love with him, and he loved her as a best friend. When we met, Kitty was coming to an end of three-year relationship with her boyfriend, and Paul was still in the middle of a two-year relationship with his boyfriend. Both husband and wife welcomed each other's lovers into the home and often spent the nights with their respective lovers in separate bedrooms. Their three young children were very much entwined with the lovers of their parents, making for one big sort-of happy family unit.

When our group first started, I was determined not to be judgmental. After all, who was I to judge how other people chose to live! I found the situations of the couples extremely bizarre, but I tried to dismiss my pre-conceived notions of what was right by my standards and tried to accept whatever made people happy. After all, what didn't work for me seemed to be working for some people, strangely enough.

Before our nucleus met, we spent hours on the telephone getting to know each other. We were all excited by the prospect of establishing a support group because we all felt so isolated living this experience. The first people I met were Cindy and Ray the week after we initially spoke. They invited me to their home, which was right in my neighborhood. After leaving them three hours later, I was shaking my head, wondering if starting the group was the right decision. Their personal life styles seemed so repugnant that I was totally turned off to the thought of being lumped categorically with them. But I was determined to start this group and decided to meet the others.

Pamela and I continued talking on the phone, and she seemed like the voice of sanity to me. She was very clear that her marriage was a disaster, but kept it together for the sake of the children and because she was raised as a staunch Catholic who didn't believe in divorce. But her religious convictions faded in time as she learned more about her husband's gay behavior. Pamela reassured me that I was right about not wanting to live with a gay man.

I formulated a name for our group, rejecting the name "WIG" as the Gay Fathers group had suggested. I wanted a name that would say what we were but also would have an acronym that we could use. After trying numerous combinations of words and letters, I devised the name "Spouses of Gays Association," which abbreviated would be "SOGA," which sounded close to SAGA...as each one of our lives had become! Even though we had not officially become a group, I knew that I should write something that we could send out to people who were interested in the group. I put together an initial statement of purpose, which was entitled, "You Are Not Alone." The text went:

> *We are a group of women that are bonded together through one common factor—our husbands are gay. We understand the confusion, pain, and heartache that you are experiencing. We don't want you to feel that you are alone, for there are thousands of other women who are living the same experience.*
>
> *Once the feeling of devastation has passed, a whole new line of questions comes to mind, starting with, "Where do I go from here?" Whether you choose to continue in your marriage or dissolve it is only a choice that you can make in the end, but we are there along the way to give support and comfort.*

We come from a vast variety of backgrounds, and our marital statuses run the gamut—some of us are married, while others are separated or divorced. Regardless of our situations, we are willing to share our experiences with you in the hope that it will help you cope better in the days ahead.

Spouses of Gays Association (SOGA) is more than just a support group. We offer help for your future with a wide spectrum of services, which include social service programs and employment or educational help. We have a 24 hour HOTLINE for emergencies and women who are willing to befriend you during this time when you will really need a friend.

There is no charge at all for our support sessions. We are doing this out of our mutual concern that women in our situation should never feel alone or isolated. All you have to do is pick up your phone and call—we'll be there for you. For future information about our meetings, please call our HOTLINE between 6— 9 p.m.

By this time, I had put together a checklist of all that was needed to start an organization. I put that in the letter I was sending out to each of the women who expressed an interest in the group. My original letter, dated December 28, 1983, stated:

Dear Friend,

Within the past month or so I have been in touch with you about the formation of a wives' support group. At the time that we spoke, you expressed an interest in such a group. This is just a note to let you know that SOGA (Spouses of Gays Association) is presently getting organized in the Philadelphia and Suburban areas. Inasmuch as this group will be far more than just a support group, there will be a great need for participation from

everyone who can spare some time—even if it is minimal. Some
of the volunteer jobs that need your help are the following:
  . Counseling
  . Hot Line
  . Liaison between resource groups
  . Research (scanning newspapers and magazines)
  . Mobilization coordinator
  . Secretarial work
  . Speakers Bureau
  . Public Relations
  . New Membership
  Even if you can spend one or two hours a month, it can greatly
boost our effectiveness. I would appreciate it if you would contact
me any evening after 9:00 p.m. or any time on the weekend to
discuss your participation in the group. Sometime in the near
future, a meeting will be scheduled for anyone who would like to
attend. In the meantime, please remember to feel free to call me
if the need is there, no matter when it is.
                      Best regards, Bonnie Kaye

I also sent out a press release to the local newspapers within two
weeks of that letter. The release dated January 16, 1984 stated:
    The Spouses of Gays Association (SOGA) announced their
formation this week in Philadelphia and surrounding suburbs.
Our purpose is to serve as a support group for women who are
married, separated, and divorced. There will be monthly meet-
ings in Philadelphia, Bucks, Montgomery, and Delaware
Counties. Besides being a support group, SOGA will also be a
social service agency to help meet the needs of its members.
Amongst services available will be counseling, employment,
educational and legal help, as well as a 24-hour HOTLINE. If

*anyone is interested in participating in the group, please call the
director, Bonnie Kaye, any evening after 6:00 p.m. A position
paper has been enclosed for your information.*

Now as I look back over this information many years later, I
realize that even though I didn't know exactly what I was doing,
my plans were quite ambitious. I realized from my own experience that emotional support would not be enough for many
women—they needed other kinds of help for their futures such
as education and employment if they were to become self-suffi-
cient and independent. The nucleus of the group, Cindy and Ray,
Kitty and Paul, and Pamela and I, gathered late in January 1984,
in my home to meet and formulate our future plans. By this
time, I had connected everyone together by phone, so we were all
excited about meeting in person. Calls from interested women
and straight/gay couples were starting to come in, and I knew
that it was time to start the support meetings.

At our initial get-together, we all decided that we would not
take a position on straight/gay marriages, for or against. We
would give support to everyone, regardless of the situation. If
people wanted to make their marriages work, that was fine. If
they decided to end their marriages, that was also fine.

Non-judgmental. That was the thought at the beginning.
After all, a support group was supposed to give support to its
members, not judge them. Obviously, after a year of weekly
meetings and conversations with hundreds of women, my own
personal opinion would change dramatically, but in the early
days, I believed in accepting everyone's situation.

Our first meeting took place on February 12, 1984 and was
held in my living room, where we held almost all of the future
meetings for the next two years. With two little children, it was

easier for me have the meetings at my home. Thirteen people showed up at our first meeting. Of course, there were the six members of the nucleus group, three more couples, and one ex-wife of a gay man. We went around the room introducing ourselves and trying to make the new people joining us very comfortable. No one was required to talk, but it seemed that after we told our stories, the new people were willing to share theirs. I had spoken to each of these people at length prior to the meeting, so I was familiar with their situations.

One couple, Laura and Donny, would become faithful members and friends. Laura had been referred to me through the Gay Fathers organization several weeks earlier when Donny decided to "come out" to her with the support of the Gay Fathers. The couple had been married for twelve years and Laura had no idea that Donny was gay. She was devastated and called me up screaming. She was very angry and vented this anger by blaming everyone remotely connected with the gay world. At first she thought that since Gay Fathers recommended me, I must be one of them. I let her yell and cry for a few minutes and then explained that I was totally sympathetic with her and understood her anger, which was much more like blind rage.

When Laura calmed down twenty minutes later, she explained that they had one daughter, age 11, and what she thought was a good marriage. Laura was raised in a blue-collar Italian family who were staunch Catholics. Donny was raised in a similar environment. They met in high school, became high school sweethearts, and married shortly after graduation.

Both Laura and Donny were working at that time, but after their daughter was born two years later, they decided that Laura would stay home and be a mother and housewife. Laura was raised in a sheltered environment and had no conception of the gay world. To the members of our group, Donny, a slight, dark-complected, handsome man, seemed effeminate in his speech and body language, but then again, we were all tuned in to homosexuality long before Laura was. We were all just as naïve in most cases until we were made aware at our husbands' convenience.

By the time of our meeting, Laura and I had spoken daily for two weeks. Donny was revealing more and more information to her each day, and her anger just kept mounting. When Donny went to the Gay Fathers for support, they were extremely accommodating. I could see from early on that I was having some deep philosophical differences with the Gay Fathers group. These differences would escalate as the weeks and months went on.

At the time of our first support meeting, Laura and Donny were not looking to split up. Donny insisted that he loved Laura and wanted to remain her husband. Laura, a voluptuous busty blonde who had never thought of being unfaithful to her husband, was not sure what she wanted to do, but she was not ready to end the marriage.

Another couple joined us, Mark and Lisa. Mark had seen our announcement of a support group in the gay newspaper and had Lisa call us for support. Mark recently revealed his homosexuality to Lisa and had just ended a relationship with a man. The couple had been married for ten years and had two young children. Lisa was devastated and needed support. Of the few men that I had met so far, Mark was the epitome of the non-stereotypical gay male. There was nothing effeminate about him. He appeared to be "straight" in every way. Mark desperately loved his wife and wanted to stay married. Ironically, the couple had a wonderful relationship. They were best friends and Mark was actively involved in the raising of his children. This was the least troublesome of marriages that I encountered over the years, and perhaps that is why Lisa found Mark's homosexuality so difficult to accept and why her feelings of betrayal were so strong.

Susan was another member who would remain with our group on a regular basis until she moved out of town a year later. I am not sure why she became so active with our group. Susan was a beautiful woman in her mid-twenties. She was attractive enough to model but had no ambition to do it. She worked as a manager in a retail-clothing store and loved her job. Susan had been married for two months when she found out that her husband was gay. Their marriage ended immediately, and she was determined to move ahead in her life but was having trouble doing it on her own. I personally couldn't understand why it would be so difficult after such a short marriage, but Susan explained that she was engaged for two years prior to marriage and felt the same sense of betrayal that we all felt. She needed to be with people who could understand what she had experienced.

One thing that I knew from my own experiences during and after my marriage was that people who had not lived through this could not understand what it does to you. They can be sympathetic and understanding in some cases, but even when they are, it isn't the same as living through the experience. Outsiders, even the most compassionate ones, can still be judgmental when you explain the situation. They commonly ask, "Didn't you suspect something was wrong before you got married?" or they question, like we ourselves question, if we are to blame for our husbands' homosexuality. Many of the women were unwilling to share this situation with family members and friends for fear of being ridiculed or rejected. Even my own family found it hard to believe that Michael could be gay, and they certainly had been exposed to numerous life experiences and not sheltered from reality. People just don't understand homosexuality enough to realize how this happens.

The other new couple that attended that first meeting was a gay male doctor and his straight wife. They came to three meetings but then stopped because they were uncomfortable with the open frankness of our meetings and felt out of place. I continued speaking to the wife by phone for several months until their marriage came to an end and her husband left.

Our first meeting started promptly at 9 p.m. and continued on long after midnight. We were all so thrilled to meet others who could understand our complex lives that we were afraid to let go. We vowed to return the following week to continue the discussions. I remember having a giant headache that night just trying to absorb what everyone was saying and trying to be a mediator to make sure that no one was judging anyone else.

As a result of the press releases that were sent out, I received a call right before the start of our support meetings from the producer of a local talk show who wanted to do an hour segment on straight/gay marriages. I thought this would be an excellent opportunity to get exposure for our group and agreed to do it. A divorced member of the Gay Fathers organization and a straight/gay married couple were also guests. I spoke about the SOGA and gave out the phone number for people to call who needed our help.

The gay father on the show, Sean, had left his marriage a number of years before. He had a teenage son and the two of them had a close personal relationship. Sean was a handsome man in his late thirties who exhibited no signs of the stereotypical femininity. He was articulate in explaining the Gay Fathers support group. He also stated that he was very open with his son about his gay lifestyle and how his son was very accepting of him. Ironically, several months down the line, I had the opportunity to have dinner with Sean and his 16-year-old son. They appeared to have an easygoing, close relationship. I took the opportunity to question the son about his feelings towards his father's homosexuality. Steve was honestly shocked when his son said that he was uncomfortable with his father's sexuality and lifestyle. He was accepting and did not love his father any less, but he was still uncomfortable. Over the years, I rarely found a teenager who was comfortable with the father's homosexuality.

Following the program, I received over thirty calls for information and help. Thanks to this exposure, our group started expanding rapidly. By March, my house was filled with between twenty and thirty people every Saturday night.

I was learning quickly. Everyone had a different situation, but all situations had a common bond—a homosexual spouse. The group was composed primarily of straight women married to gay men; however, I started receiving calls from straight men married to lesbian women. Although I didn't know the effects of these dynamics, I quickly learned thanks to several men that started attending our sessions.

The first male to join our group was Arnie. Some of the women in the group, including me, developed a crush on him. Arnie wasn't particularly handsome or charming. He was an average-looking guy who was thirty pounds overweight. This was not surprising because he was a chef in a major Philadelphia hotel. But there was something very kind and good about Arnie.

He represented the ideal man we were seeking in life. He was caring, understanding, and gentle—all of the qualities we wanted in a husband. He was overly sympathetic to his wife, who had left him for another woman. They had been married for four years after a two-year courtship in college. Arnie's wife, Joan, had questioned her sexuality since adolescence, but never dealt with it prior to the marriage. When she decided to act on her feelings, Arnie was totally supportive even though he was emotionally destroyed. Joan started going to lesbian bars, and within a few weeks, met a woman who began a relationship with her. Arnie agreed to give Joan time to see if this was really what she wanted.

When the lesbian relationship ended after several months, Joan stated that she was not comfortable in the lesbian world and wanted to remain married. Arnie was elated because he thought that Joan "got it out of her system," and believed their marriage would be back on track after a short readjustment period. Within months, Joan found herself going back to the lesbian bars. She told Arnie that she was not looking to meet anyone, but she felt comfortable in that setting and only wanted to make friends. Arnie wanted to believe this was true. He was hoping against hope that Joan would realize that she was not part of the lesbian world.

Of course, this did not happen. At the time that Arnie joined us, Joan had moved out and was living with a lover. He spoke with her every few days, trying to be understanding but still wanting her back. He was even willing to accept the fact that she needed female companionship, emotional and sexual, if she was willing to stay married to him.

Most of us go through the stage of "how much can I live with to keep my marriage together?" in the beginning when we find out. The thought of breaking up a marriage, even a bad marriage, is difficult, especially when children are involved.

When I first suspected Michael of being gay or bisexual, I was repulsed by the thought, but mentally, I envisioned all of the different case scenarios I could live with. One evening during the third year of our marriage, I recall a conversation we had. I was very careful never to outwardly accuse him of being gay because I remembered his volatile reaction when I first questioned him prior to our marriage. By this time, I knew that he had an interest in men, and I was even able to tell the type that appealed to him. In this conversation, I remember saying, "If you have the need to act on any feelings you may have, and once every six months or so you're not home for a few hours and I don't have to know about it, I can live with it."

I had things "wrapped up" into a neat package that was doable to me. I wasn't happy about it, but if I didn't have to know about it, I could keep my miserable marriage intact. It's amazing how little people are willing to settle for in life, especially when their self-esteem is beaten down. Unfortunately, homosexuality is not something that can be contained or controlled, but I didn't understand this or much else during my marriage.

Arnie finally accepted that Joan was not going to work out as his wife although he still hung on to some hope. This was because Joan kept running back to him every time a relationship didn't work out. After the fifth time, he knew that he was an emotional safety net for her and told her that she couldn't run back again.

Several other straight men with lesbian wives came to our group over the years, but they usually did not stay for more than a few sessions. It seems like men have an easier time moving ahead in their lives than women do, but they also have the same feelings of sexual inadequacy that the straight wives have, if not more so. In general, men's sexual egos are very fragile. No man wants to feel like he is a failure sexually. When your wife turns to other women and away from you, it is natural to start questioning your ability as a lover. One thing the meetings accomplished was helping to reassure the straight husband that the problem was not his, but rather his wife's.

It appeared that straight men have an easier time dealing with their wives' lesbianism for several reasons. Generally speaking, men are not as emotional as women are or at least are socialized not to be. Also, a man can deal better with visualizing his wife with another woman than a woman can visualizing her husband with another man. After all, most men fantasize about two women being together so the whole concept is somewhat exotic and erotic. However, the reality is different than the fantasy, and the husbands are devastated when this happens for more than just a casual sexual fantasy fulfillment. But they seem to have an easier time moving on with their lives. In most of the cases that I have dealt with, the mother remains the primary caretaker of the children. The man has more time to have a social life and can readjust more easily to being single again.

There were hundreds of stories that were told that first year, and the overwhelming majority of them were unhappy ones. Some were extremely strange even by my standards, but once again, I tried to look at this as a learning experience and not be judgmental.

One of the problems that seemed to prevail in straight/gay marriages was the lack of honesty of the gay partner to the straight spouse. I started to have a problem with the fact that so many married gay men would not be truthful with their wives until they were ready to be honest. I spoke to women who spent thousands of dollars and hundreds of hours going to gynecologists and therapists looking for a problem that was not theirs to find. They couldn't understand why their husbands were not interested in them sexually and believed there must be something wrong with them. I know how this tears you up inside, continually searching for the answer of what you are doing wrong and losing your self-confidence as a woman.

I understood the needs of the straight spouse only too well because I was in the situation and knew the effects. But I still didn't understand the feelings of our gay husbands or the gay community because my only real exposure was to the men who participated in our support meetings. I decided the only way I could really understand things better was to do more research. And what better way to do this than first hand experience!

The gay husbands in our group agreed that the gay bars were a natural place for gay men to congregate. A few of them volunteered to take me to a few clubs to see what goes on there. I agreed to go, partly out of personal curiosity and partly because of professional learning. Donny and Ray accompanied me to my first gay bar. At that time, there were seven gay bars in the center of town. I remember feeling paralyzed as I walked into the largest of bars at that time, Equis. There was a jumbo-sized bouncer sitting by the door in case anyone thought about starting trouble. At that time, gay-bashing in the inner cities across America was on the rise, and Philadelphia was no exception. There were terrible incidents of violence against gay men on the streets when they were leaving the gay clubs, and bouncers served as a deterrent for problems inside the clubs.

When you walked inside the room, there was a long bar and a number of smaller tables with televisions overhead. It didn't look much different than a regular bar. There were a few guys seated at the bar hanging on to each other, but not many. We walked up a flight of steps into the dance area. This was a culture shock for me. Dozens of men were dancing with each other and the sight of this kept me numb. I felt as if my feet were stuck to the floor and couldn't move. I couldn't talk, and I was standing by myself because Donny and Ray joined the dance floor and began dancing to the song, "It's Raining Men," a big hit in the gay bars at that time. Both men encouraged me to join them dancing, but there was no way that this would happen. I was sickened by the reality of the images and my only thought was to run out of there. Finally my escorts agreed to leave with me, knowing that nothing they could say or do would make me feel comfortable.

Perhaps if I had not been so close to the situation by having a gay husband I would have not reacted that way. But being there was like opening up a raw wound for me. Until now, homosexuality was just hearsay from people I knew, books I read, and members of our group. Seeing hundreds of men in this environment dancing, hugging, kissing, making out, and fondling each other was more than I could mentally process. It brought back every feeling of revulsion that I had during my own marriage. I went home that night emotionally drained and sickened. When Donny and Ray asked me to go out with them the following week to a different bar, I backed out with some made-up excuse.

They knew I was unable to cope with the bar scene, but insisted they were going to take me to a place that I would enjoy. They told me about a piano bar where many straight people went. I was a music lover and they thought that would be more to my liking. I reluctantly agreed to go but made them promise to leave within one hour if I was not comfortable.

My friends were right. This bar was relatively non-threatening compared to the other one. When you walked in, there was a large grand piano with bar stools lined up around it. There were both men and women singing along with the piano player, some of whom I learned later were professional singers. When theater tours came from out of town to perform, they often visited this bar after their shows to relax and unwind by singing. There was a large bar next to the piano where people sat and drank. The next level had the dance floor, which I avoided at all cost because of my discomfort with it.

I started going to the piano bar once a week and became friendly with some of the regulars there. It's funny how people can become accustomed to almost anything. After a number of weeks, it didn't even bother me when I saw two men embracing. It started looking normal to me. I was not looking to enjoy a night out when I went to the bar, but rather I was still looking to learn about the gay culture. I always took the opportunity to talk to whoever was willing to talk.

Some of the men wanted nothing to do with a straight woman who was looking for information. They had come to enjoy themselves and did not want to be hassled. But others were very willing to talk to me about a wide variety of subjects. I learned about the hardships of being gay in a world that is non-accepting and prejudiced. I learned about men whose families had cut them off when they learned of their homosexuality. I heard so many sad love stories in the bar that I started to think that there was no such thing as a happy gay relationship.

I learned about a value system that was different than the straight world. It seemed as though gay relationships were short-lived and very temporary. When I met men who had been together for a number of years with a partner, it was never a monogamous relationship. And both partners seemed to be fine with this because they didn't equate sex and love together. In 1984, AIDS was becoming a national epidemic in the gay community, and yet, the men I spoke to had a very careless attitude, believing it couldn't happen to them. It took me a long time to understand why the gay community was so sexually oriented, but I learned to understand that man by nature is very sexual. Men who are gay just cut to the chase and get down to business. In the straight community, the sexual needs of men may be the same, but the majority of women have different needs, so the story is acted out differently.

Through my several years of immersion into the periphery of the gay community, I came to feel a deep sense of sorrow for gay men who so desperately wanted the same sense of security that the straight world relationships offered but were seldom achieved. Lots of heartaches, heartbreak, and self-destruction. Several of the friends I made during this time passed away from AIDS, including one of the founding couples' husbands, Paul. At the time of his death, he and Kitty had split up and gone their separate ways. The couple that swore they could stay together forever and lead their open lives together eventually fell apart when Paul met the right man who didn't like having Kitty as part of the relationship. That right man caused Paul's eventual death.

During this period, I felt like a stranger in a strange land. I tried my best to comprehend the psyche of the average gay male, but I fell short of really understanding. I was trying to be open-minded about a lifestyle that did not make sense to me. It wasn't the sexual aspect of man with man that I couldn't accept. In fact, I believe that I was more sympathetic and empathetic about homosexuality that most people I have ever met to this day. What I found disturbing was the difference in moral values. I have my own thinking about this that has never been widely discussed in open circles. It was accepted that gay men could lead a double life without informing their wives until they felt the need to do so without concern for what this might be doing to the partner that they claimed to love. I didn't understand why honesty, the basis of a relationship, was not the primary goal. I came to believe that gay people find it easier to lie than straight people.

Now, please don't misunderstand me—this is not an innate character flaw, but rather the result of a society that forces people to lie about what they are, lest they be condemned. When people feel forced to lie about who and what they are, they become conditioned to living a lie. That is why I believe it is easy for a gay man to lie about his sexuality in his marriage—he's been lying about it for years to the rest of the world.

Chapter 7

And Suffer the Children…

No one is more vulnerable than the innocent children that are born into straight/gay marriages. All children who come from unstable homes suffer, but often these children suffer more because they have additional problems to contend with than others.

There are several issues that are different with children from straight/gay marriages than in traditional marriages. The most important worry that straight wives have is wondering if there is an increased chance of their children being gay because of the gay father. This seems to be a reality from the statistics that I have compiled and studied over the years. As I mentioned earlier in Chapter 2, there is a higher occurrence of gay children born into straight/gay marriages. If you accept that homosexuality results from genetics, then this makes sense. It is estimated that 10% of the general population is homosexual. From less confirmed studies that have taken place, this statistic moves up to as high as 18% when a child has one gay parent.

I have heard debates through the years that this is due to role modeling by the gay parent, but I don't believe that to be true. If this was the case, why aren't all of the children in the family gay?

Also, there are numerous gay fathers who never reveal their homosexuality and appear to be the most macho guys in the world. Whatever the reason, this is a real situation that families have to deal with.

The results can become very disheartening if the straight wife does not get past her homophobic feelings. If she is always downgrading gays, her gay child will find him/herself in the same situation as the gay father, trying to escape his/her homosexuality and spending years going through self-hatred and denial.

Another problem that children of gay parents face is the constant questioning of their sexuality throughout adolescence. The teenage years are the most difficult ones to deal with sexuality. Knowing that a parent is gay weighs heavily on the minds of teenagers who wonder whether this has been passed down to them. Even when the teenager is not gay, he or she fears that progression in age will lead to being gay. I have interviewed and counseled twenty-seven daughters of gay men who knew their fathers were gay prior to adolescence. The overwhelming majority suffered with this knowledge creating a situation where they became promiscuous to prove to themselves that they were straight. Their sexual activities started at a young age, as if they believed that having sex with men would make them straight.

Six of the twenty-seven daughters were lesbians and came to terms with it late in their teenage years or in early adulthood. These six women knew that they were different at a young age, but they were hoping that homosexuality was not what made them different. This is why they started having sexual relations with boys when they were between the ages of 13 and 15. Over time they were able to successfully accept their sexuality.

Ironically, two of these women's gay fathers could not accept them being lesbians.

Most of the other females I spoke to claimed that they started having sexual relations long before they were ready just to make sure that they were "normal." This created more anguish because if they didn't enjoy the sex, they started to question if they were gay. They were too young to understand that teenage sex is often not fulfilling due to the inexperience of their male sex partners and the fact that their bodies and hormones are not fully developed.

Over time, I was able to find fifteen sons of gay men who were willing to discuss their emotions and feelings with me about their adolescent years. Eleven of the fifteen claimed to be straight, and one identified himself as bisexual. It seems as if the males had a much more difficult time dealing with their sexuality than the females. This was because of the way that society is socialized. Society is less accepting of a gay male than a lesbian female. It is also not unusual for adolescent boys to take part in some form of homosexual experimentation at least once, whether it be masturbating with a group of friends or fondling genitals of youthful playmates.

While other males just chalk it up to experimentation and rarely think about it again, sons of gay men think about it often, worrying that they are like their fathers. All of the sons told me that they became sexually active with girls at a young age to try to reassure themselves that they were straight, similarly the way that daughters of gay fathers reacted.

It was interesting to also note that the females were able to deal with their fathers' gay relationships much more easily than the sons were. Even if the daughters were not happy about seeing their fathers embracing a male lover, it didn't seem to put that much of a strain on the father-daughter relationships. The males, on the other hand, felt uncomfortable and even intimidated by their fathers' relationships once they reached adolescence, even if they knew the father's significant other prior to their teenage years. It is important to note that once most of the sons became adults, they were able to deal with their fathers' lifestyles better. By this time, they were secure in their own sexuality so it was easier to be accepting of their fathers and their fathers' lovers.

The children of the gay fathers had different feelings based on how their fathers handled their homosexuality and how they interacted with the children in general. Also, they were influenced by their mothers' reactions to their fathers' homosexuality.

Each person had a different level of acceptance. Some children could deal with the situation on an intellectual level, but when a father became involved in an actual relationship, the child was not able to deal with it. In straight relationships, the children may reject the new woman or man friend that a parent becomes involved with, but this is usually due to personality differences or jealousy on the part of the child. With a gay father, the rejection goes far beyond that point. It is not comfortable to see a father holding and caressing another man. It hits a negative cord in the brain as if it is something unnatural. Plus, with all of the homophobia in the world, we are taught from an early age that this imaging is deviant.

Children with gay fathers are usually ultra-secretive about their fathers' sexual identities. Some of the children of gay fathers that I've known have told me horror stories about other kids' reactions to them. This included acts of violence perpetrated by other teens, isolation from homes of friends, and refusal to be allowed to date peers by parents of the peers.

When I met the first members of my support group, Cindy and Ray, I also met their three children, Lori, 21; Marla, 19; and David, 16. Cindy's daughters were very outgoing like their parents and outspoken about the cruelty they suffered when people learned their father was gay.

Ray used to pick up men by hanging out in men's bathrooms in local department stores. He was very direct in his approach with anyone whom he thought might be interested in having a sexual encounter. Over the years, classmates of Lori and Marla frequently saw Ray pursuing men and concluded that their father was "a faggot," as he was called by the teenage boys who kept running into him in the department stores.

Both girls were beaten up repeatedly by high school peers who deemed them deviant because of their father. Their names were scrawled in the boys' bathrooms as being pigs and whores. In truth, both girls were very promiscuous because they wanted to make sure that they were straight and not gay. They needed to prove to themselves that they were not like their father. Their younger brother had an easier time because he was adopted and didn't worry about the genetic pool. He also entered high school after his sisters had graduated; people didn't realize who his sisters and father were.

Other children of gay fathers had similar experiences. They were ostracized, belittled, called names, isolated from their peers, labeled as gay when they weren't, etc. It's hard to believe that people are so ignorant, but it is true.

I will share an incident that happened when my children were young that forced me to stop doing television appearances. At that time, my son was in nursery school and my daughter was in kindergarten in a private school. I had done several national talk shows and various local shows about straight/gay marriages. I knew from the other members of my group that I was on a limited time line. Once my children were in regular public school the following year, I would not be able to appear on these shows anymore because they would suffer from the public backlash.

When the Sally Jessie Raphael Show producers asked me to appear on her show in 1986, I was leery because of my children. I explained my apprehension to the producer, but she reminded me that in Philadelphia at that time, the show was on at 5:00 a.m., even though it was shown on primetime morning hours throughout the rest of the country. She convinced me that thousands of people could be helped and minimized any possibility of damage to my children because of the remote hour of the local morning broadcast. I suppose I justified this in my own mind because I wanted to get the message to as many people as possible. Every time I did a television show, hundreds of letters poured in from women who were grateful for my message because they were living in an isolated hell with no one who understood their situation.

I went to St. Louis where the show was filmed. People always ask me if these shows pay you to be a guest. To my knowledge, they don't; however, they pay your travel, hotel, and food expenses. It gives people the chance to promote whatever causes they may be championing. Of course, over the years, some of the legitimate talk shows have turned into circuses for everyone and his brother who are seeking their fifteen minutes of fame. But in the 1980s, shows like Donahue, Oprah, and Sally were informational and informative and helped millions of people with different problems ranging from rare medical conditions to social ills.

Sally Jessie Raphael was a lovely person. She spent a few moments with me before the show to try to put me at ease. There was just one other guest on her show, and I had ample opportunity throughout the hour to talk about straight/gay marriages. As anticipated, I received hundreds of letters from all over the country from women in similar situations who finally understood what was going on in their marriages.

When the show was broadcast in Philadelphia, no one I knew mentioned to me that they had seen it, so I felt confident that there would be no repercussions. Several months later, my son, Alex, needed surgery because he had an infected lymph node. He was out of nursery school for two weeks. Before he returned, I received a call from the director of the school. She compassionately informed me that the parents of the children in Alex's class had petitioned for him not to be allowed to return. They based this on the conclusion that Alex had AIDS. One of the mothers had seen me on the Sally show, so she knew that Alex had a gay father. Then she found out that he was in the hospital for surgery and put the two pieces of information together concluding that if Alex had a gay father and was in the hospital, he must have AIDS.

In 1986, there was still a lot of unknown and misinformation about AIDS. People thought that you could contract AIDS just from breathing in the same air that an infected person was breathing. This one mother flamed the fires of the other mothers telling them that their children were at risk by playing with or sitting next to Alex in the same classroom.

Needless to say, I was horrified. The school administrator told the parents that they could take their children out of school, but she would not have Alex removed. I volunteered to remove Alex rather than have the school suffer, but the teachers were adamant that they would not be blackmailed by a modern-day witchhunt. This was my wake-up call. That was the last public program I appeared on, even though I had numerous offers from other top rated shows to be a guest. I knew if my children would be stigmatized at such a young age, they would go through school without friends and become the victims of ignorant parents and classmates.

I was always sympathetic with women whose husbands were openly gay in front of the children. They were not comfortable with their children watching their ex-husbands with other male lovers embracing and kissing. I understood that discomfort because I would have felt the same. Michael was involved with different men over the years, but he never demonstrated his affection for his partners in front of the children. He did not take them to gay events, gay meetings, gay father picnics, etc. Some fathers were insistent that their children attend these functions, creating a problem between the mothers and the gay fathers. If Michael had been that way, it would have put a tremendous strain on my relationship with him and the children's relationships with him.

I tried to be fair in my judgments of these matters. I understood the gay father's need to validate his new lifestyle. He had finally come to terms with his homosexuality and he was proud of what he was. He believed that his children should also be just as accepting of his lifestyle. He was tired of hiding and pretending and now that he was ready to be honest, he wanted to share that information with his children. He wanted his children to love him for who he was, even if it was different than what the children expected.

Of course, I understood the rage of the straight mother who not only had to contend with the news that her husband was gay, but was now left as a single parent with broken dreams and a broken marriage. Over time, many of these women could accept that their husbands were gay, but they did not want their children being dragged into the gay world. They couldn't understand why their ex-husbands who only had a few hours a week with the children couldn't spend quality time with them outside the gay community. They also felt that the gay lifestyle was being imposed on their children whether the children liked it or not.

Some mothers were fearful that other gay men would molest their children, and although I tried to reassure them that this was not the case, it often became a difficult argument. These stories were always fueled by groups like NAMBLA (National Association for Man-Boy Love) that promoted sex with children. Even though I showed evidence that there were straight groups with the same ideology, it didn't make much of an argument when there was so much publicity going on at the time about gay men wanting to molest boys.

I have met numerous gay men who are totally opposed to groups like NAMBLA. The thought of man-boy love is equally appalling to these gay men as it is to society in general. However, there is a lack of loud opposition on their part and I conclude this is because there are differences in the gay community's way of viewing the age of consenting sexuality. I did not find it uncommon for gay men to accept the concept of men having sex with teenage boys. Many of them projected back to their own teenage years when they wanted sex and felt it was perfectly normal to engage in it with an older, more experienced man.

Almost every gay man I have spoken to over the years admits to having a sexual encounter with an older man while he was a teenager. They also didn't feel that there was anything wrong or abnormal about it. Although this certainly happens with straight people, it does not happen nearly as often or is it classified as acceptable. In the straight world, people can accept teenagers having sex with other teens; but the thought of teenage girls or boys having sex with adults ten or more years older than them is not condoned. Even in a society where there is a double standard for females and males concerning sexual activity, it is still not socially acceptable for a teenage boy to be seduced by an older woman. Recently a female schoolteacher was jailed for having sex with a thirteen-year-old teenage boy while having his baby. Society has its limits, and once those limits are surpassed, there is little sympathy or understanding.

The issue of a gay parent is difficult enough for the gay parent and straight spouse to deal with. How much more difficult it must be for the child to deal with. The most important consideration for both parents is to think of the needs of the child first. For instance, if a child is uncomfortable with a father's homosexuality, the father should avoid thrusting the child into the gay arena. I knew gay fathers who insisted that their children participate in gay rights marches and rallies and carry signs with slogans such as "We Love Our Gay Fathers." Now this may look great for the cameras, but it makes the child very uncomfortable, fearing that peers in school may see the picture. Some children have no problem with their fathers being gay, but rather the insistence that the gay father has to announce it wherever he goes or when he is openly participating in the gay community. Once again, this leads to the issue of how the gay father handles his sexuality in front of the children.

I have seen bitter court battles with mothers fighting for sole custody and supervised visitation with the gay father because they are unable to deal with their ex-husbands' lifestyles. The fathers, on the other hand, are not willing to compromise when it comes to the needs of the children. They believe they can no longer live a lie and once they are involved in a relationship, they do not want to hide it from their children.

One gay couple, Don and Jack, tried to abide by the wishes of Don's ex-wife, Phyllis. Don was a strapping man of 6 feet four inches, who weighed 280 pounds. He had left Phyllis two years earlier after becoming involved with Jack, a slight black man who was half his size in weight, and at least one foot shorter in height. Don and Phyllis were both in their mid-thirties when their marriage ended. Phyllis was shocked when Don revealed that he was gay because he was the typical "macho" jock that she always worried would cheat with women.

Don had a strong personality and he was always flirting with the women. He later revealed that he was a flirt, but he was acting just to throw off anyone's suspicion. Don first knew that he was gay when he was in his teens. He had numerous sexual encounters with males. But the family pressure for a wife, children, business, home in the suburbs, etc. was intense, so he gave up the thoughts of leading a gay life. He met Phyllis when they were in their third year of college. Phyllis also had a strong personality, unlike the majority of other wives of gay men that I have met through the years. The two became fast friends because they shared numerous interests from politics to theater. After graduation from college, they married.

The first few years of the marriage were great. They loved each other's company, and even though their sex life was less than perfect, neither one of them cared that much about it. Phyllis had limited lovers before marriage, and she believed that marriage was the foundation for family and security. Sex was not a criterion to base a marriage on. Don performed sex with Phyllis as often as he thought he had to, which was usually once a month. He appreciated that fact that Phyllis was not one of those "nagging nymphos" as he called it. She was a "good wife" to him in that respect. What he didn't realize was that Phyllis thought he was unsatisfying in bed, which is why she didn't nag him. Her philosophy was that life was about a lot more than sex. It was about family and possessions, both of which Don could provide for her.

Don's family owned a successful furniture business that he inherited upon his college graduation. Phyllis became the mother of two children, Arlene and Russ, who were born two years apart, starting two years after the marriage. Don was a doting father and Phyllis was a controlling, but devoted, mother. They developed friendships with numerous couples who had children, and it was a weekly ritual to spend the weekends with at least two or three of these couples.

Don and Phyllis moved to a beautiful home on the Main Line on their five-year anniversary, and a number of their couple friends moved into the same development. To an outsider, this was the perfect family unit. A loving couple, two smart, adorable children, a house in the suburbs, great friends, a thriving business. Life was almost perfect—or at least Phyllis and the children thought it was.

Actually, Don was happy too. He and Phyllis were the best of friends. She never questioned him when he went out with the "guys." Of course, she was never suspicious that he was out having sex with the "guys."

Phyllis met Jack, the lust of Don's life, several years before the split-up. Don told her that Jack was the new assistant manager for the furniture store and the hardest worker that the store ever had. Jack was quiet but very likeable. Or maybe he just seemed quiet because Don was so overbearing. He was a frequent visitor in their household, and in time, Phyllis and the kids treated him like a member of the family.

Don and Phyllis could have led their lives like this for years, but Jack couldn't. He was tired of feeling like the third member of a crowd. Don had promised that in time, when the kids were older, he would tell Phyllis the truth and leave his happy home for a happier life with Jack. At the time, Jack thought he could deal with the arrangement, but after two years, he no longer could. He gave Don the ultimatum— "choose me or Phyllis, but you can't have both." With no choice but to choose, Don picked Jack.

Telling Phyllis the truth was the hardest thing that Don ever had to do in his life. He knew that his wife would not take this news well, and he also knew that there would be severe repercussions. But Don also knew that he had to be true to himself. He was very much in love with Jack and couldn't imagine life without him.

For weeks, Don practiced different ways to reveal this secret to his wife. Nothing sounded right because there was no way to soften the blow of the message. Don couldn't find the courage to have this kind of confrontation with Phyllis. In the end, he left her a letter explaining why he was leaving and just left.

Phyllis not only felt like a woman scorned but also like a woman burned. After twelve years of marriage, Don chose to leave her for a black man—a man who had spent countless times in their home with Phyllis treating him like a family member. She thought their perfect lives had been nothing more than a lie—a cover for the world to see. She felt used and violated. She didn't like being the brunt of this joke.

Don gave Phyllis the house, the car, a large support payment, and anything else she wanted that money could buy to try to make up for what he couldn't give her emotionally. Phyllis went on a buying spree, spending thousands of dollars to help her feel better about her life. Somehow, the usual high she always felt from spending didn't seem quite as exhilarating anymore.

During their first two months of separation, there was no verbal contact. Phyllis retained a lawyer within 24 hours and all communication was done by law firms. Don felt guilty for hurting his family, so he didn't pursue the issue of visitation rights in the beginning. Arlene was ten years old and Russ was eight at the time their father left. Phyllis didn't tell them the truth. She had no intention of informing her children that their father left her for a black man.

In spite of Don's guilt, he was happier than he had ever been during his marriage to Phyllis. Jack was his soulmate, his best friend, and his lover. Sex was exciting and fulfilling for the first time in his life. He never regretted making his decision to leave. Once they were on their own, Don and Jack decided to join a gay organization called Black and White Men Together. This was an organization where white men and black men who were attracted to each other could meet, socialize, politicize, and party. It didn't take long for Don and Jack to become leaders in the group.

Even though Jack was the love of Don's life, they both had sexual relationships with other men. Sometimes they did it together, sometimes separately. They both claimed that love had nothing to do with sexual activity. This seems to be an underlying philosophy in the gay community. I am not judging it, just acknowledging it.

After the first few months of separation passed, Don made a request to have the children stay with him and Jack one evening a week and every other weekend. Phyllis said the only way that she would allow this was if Don and Jack slept in separate bedrooms so that the kids would think they were roommates and not lovers.

This worked for Don and he felt it was the right thing to do for the children. For the first few months of visitation, there was no conflict.

One evening after a visitation, Arlene casually mentioned to her mother that when she woke up in the middle of the night and went into her father's bedroom, Uncle Jack was sleeping "naked" with him. Phyllis hit the roof. She felt sick to her stomach, imagining the worst scenario possible. When the children went to sleep, she phoned Don and called him every filthy name she could think of. Don apologized and promised it wouldn't happen again. Phyllis said she would never allow the children to sleep there again if it did happen. As the months wore on, Jack became annoyed that he had to sleep alone on the night that the kids were there. He felt as if they had become one big happy family unit and resented that fact that he had to pretend to be something he wasn't to appease Phyllis. This created tension between Don and Jack, and Jack threatened to end the relationship if Don didn't abide by his wishes. By that time, Don agreed that his sleeping arrangement was none of Phyllis's business. Jack was Don's true love of a lifetime and he wasn't about to sacrifice that for a nagging ex-wife. Anyway, his children loved Jack, and Don was convinced that they couldn't care less about who slept where. Although Don and Jack didn't flaunt their arrangements, they stopped hiding it.

Since Phyllis felt the need to cross-examine the children upon their arrival home on their weekends away, it didn't take long for her to find out about the new sleeping arrangements. At that point, she was determined to keep the children away from what she referred to as "insanity." She refused to allow any further overnight visits or even day visits. Don was infuriated and decided to take legal action.

Phyllis called in a panel of psychologists on behalf of the children, who all claimed that there could definitely be damage to the children's emotional state by being exposed to this kind of environment. Don was not expecting this attack and came unprepared. The court granted Don supervised visitation once every two weeks under the care of a social worker in a public place. In the 1980's, the political climate towards gay couples was less than positive, and courts often gave full rights to the straight mothers. Phyllis also had in her favor that Don and Jack were now the leaders of an organization called Black and White Men Together. The organization was a social/political group that focused on interracial gay relationships. Now it was not uncommon to have the house filled with male couples when the children were visiting, many of which were in compromising positions in front of the children.

These supervised visits continued for years until the children were old enough to determine if they wanted to spend more time with their father. By the time they were able to make the decision, it was too late. Their father died from AIDS.

When to the tell the children and who should tell the children are life-affecting issues and should be well thought out with all of the ramifications that can result from this news. Either parent might be anxious to tell the child for his or her own personal reasons, but it doesn't mean that the time is right for the child.

Is there ever a right time? Or rather, is there ever a good time? It depends on the maturity of your children and their ability to process this information. From my experience and the experiences of so many others in this situation, I would say that the period of adolescence is perhaps the least opportune time.

For instance, my daughter was more worldly and mature than my son, and I felt the need to tell her about her dad at an earlier age. Her father was not ready to tell her, and this created a terrible rift between us that lasted for almost a year. He felt it should have been his place to explain this to her when he was ready. I wanted him to tell her because by the time she was twelve years old, she was finding things in his house, including gay magazines and movies. Michael was also involved in a relationship and my daughter would question why her dad was sleeping with another man.

He didn't want to tell her, but I didn't want her to think that the material she was finding in his home was the way of the world. I didn't want her getting distorted images of what sexuality was supposed to be like for her. Since Michael wouldn't tell her, I felt I had to tell her.

I am often asked what is the best way to approach children with this news. I think the way I approached it was with sensitivity and caring. There was no name calling—no aggressive accusations pointing a finger of blame. I sat my daughter, Stephanie, down and told her that we needed to have an important conversation.

I remember telling her that all people were born different, and that no two people are the same. Some people have blue eyes, some have brown. Some people have blonde hair, while others have brown and red. Some people have white skin, while others have brown skin. Most people are born straight and fall in love with people of the opposite sex. But some are born gay and fall in love with people of the same sex. I asked her if she knew any gay people. At that point, she had met some of my gay friends over the years and was able to name them. I never hid my gay friends' sexuality from my children because I didn't believe that I should have to lie about it if my friends were comfortable with their sexuality.

I asked Stephanie if she knew anybody who was gay besides my friends and she mentioned a couple of friends of Michael were gay. I explored her feelings about "gay" to see if she felt any negativity. I had tried my best over the years to raise my children in an environment of compassion and understanding for anyone who was different than they were because of my personal beliefs and convictions. As a result of this, my daughter was extremely liberal in her thinking about others and had no difficulty with someone because of his or her sexuality.

Having friends who are gay is much different than having a parent that is gay. The hard part was making the transition between people Stephanie knew were gay and bridging that over to "your father is gay." After the words came out, they could never be taken back, and I knew that Stephanie's life would change forever after that information was revealed.

I emphasized the need to keep that information confidential because her peers would not be nearly as understanding as she was. Many people were ignorant when it came to homosexuality, and they would take it out on her if they found out. I had already learned the lessons of horrors from too many other children with gay fathers. I also asked Stephanie not to let her father know that I had told her about his sexuality because I knew he would be very angry. For six months, she kept this secret, but then she told her father that she knew.

At the age of twelve, Stephanie felt sorry for her father after finding out he was gay. It didn't bother her at that point as it would later on in her teens. She told her father because she wanted him to know that she loved him no matter what.

Needless to say, that was the one time in our relationship that Michael was the angriest at me. I never felt his anger and contempt the way I did on that day or over the next year while he refused to talk to me. And yet, I knew I had no choice but to tell our daughter.

Would I have told her under all circumstances? No. If Michael had not kept the evidence around or been involved in a relationship, I don't feel that there is a need to know. I have met some men through the years who never revealed their homosexuality to their children because they were leading visibly straight lives without suspicion. In that situation, why rock the boat? Of course, this is a decision that the gay father needs to make depending on his comfort level with being gay.

I once met a man, Joe, who had left his wife when his children were teenagers because he could no longer live the straight lie. He told his wife, Rosa, the truth, and they both agreed for the sake of the children that it was better to keep that information private between themselves. Joe promised Rosa that he would never do anything to embarrass her or the children. If he had a relationship, the children would never meet the person, and there would never be any way for their three children to tell. It sounded like a feasible game plan.

Ironically, Joe and Rosa's oldest son, Vincent, was gay. He struggled with his homosexuality throughout his teenage years, fearing that if his family found out, he would be shunned. The family was active in their church where there was not much acceptance for homosexuality. Vince had always heard the not-so-subtle messages that gay was a sin. This added even more to his confusion about himself.

Vince had a solid relationship with Joe. As the first and oldest son, there had been a strong bond developed since birth. Joe knew his son was struggling with something, but was unable to get the information out of him. Joe told Vince that he could tell him anything—nothing could change his love for his son. But Vince was too hung up on fears of rejection to ever discuss it.

One morning, Rosa waited for Vince to come down to breakfast before school. When he didn't, she went into his room, assuming he had overslept. She found her son unconscious with a note. The note read, "Dear Mom and Dad, I could no longer live with the truth that I am gay knowing how it would destroy both of you. It is just easier to destroy myself. I love you, Vince."

Rosa started screaming and shaking Vince, but he did not wake up. She called 911 and then Joe, and they all were in the hospital within twelve minutes. Vince had taken a bottle of over-the-counter sleeping pills the night before but miraculously survived. Joe broke down hysterically crying and blaming himself for his son's homosexuality. Rosa also blamed Joe because she was so distraught at the moment.

When Vince regained consciousness, Rosa and Joe embraced him and explained that they loved him more than ever, and that Joe had something to reveal to him. Joe then told him the truth about his own sexuality. Although Vince felt relieved to know that his parents still loved him, he felt little comfort in the news that his father was gay. Vince also blamed his father for his homosexuality, and he couldn't understand why a gay man would want to produce children.

The family went for family counseling over the next eight months, and all of them learned to be open and honest in dealing with their feelings. In time, Vince understood why his father didn't reveal his secret—he was as fearful of rejection as his son was. Vince joined a support group for gay teenagers and in time was able to accept himself.

It is not unusual for teenagers to resent the fact that their fathers are gay, even if they grew up knowing the truth or were told prior to adolescence. Almost every teenager resents having a gay father on some level depending on the responsibility or lack of it on the part of the father.

One young lady, Gina, told me that her father repulsed her because he would hit on the guys she was bringing home. He would deny any such action, but she lost at least five young men in her life this way. After that, she secretly dated until she moved out of her house at the age of 18. I have heard similar stories from other daughters of gay fathers who are terrified about introducing their fathers to their boyfriends. They also share the fear of revealing their fathers' sexuality to boyfriends.

As I mentioned earlier in the chapter, there are often repercussions from parents who find out that their child is going with someone who has a gay father. Several of the daughters of gay fathers that I counseled told of relationships being destroyed by the pressures of the parents of their boyfriends once they learned that the girls' fathers were gay.

There are no easy answers to any of these issues. The most important advice is to learn to communicate. If your husband is gay, it is vitally important to have a heart-to-heart conversation about how and when to reveal this information to the children. The worst thing is for parents to use this information as a weapon against each other. I have heard wives threaten, "If he doesn't do this or that, I'm telling the kids that they have a faggot for a father." Who is the winner here? No one.

Children will have a difficult enough time dealing with this information, even if it comes out in a loving, accepting way. Teenagers are very homophobic by nature, and no one wants to be mocked or ostracized while they are growing up. This news changes lives because it creates secrets in the child, or sometimes even lies. It also creates an element of fear that the news will be revealed.

Parents must always keep in mind the need for safety and security of the children over their own needs of anger and revenge. As difficult as this may be, a straight mother should not discuss her own homophobic feelings with the children. For better or worse, this is the father of your child. What parents don't understand in general, not just relating to being married to someone gay, is that children always believe that they are made up of two parts—their mother and father. If they know that something is a problem with either parent, they believe that there is something wrong within them and this lowers their sense of self-esteem.

If a mother downgrades the father because of his homosexuality, this will leave doubts within the children. They will start believing that there is something wrong within them, often causing behavior that is destructive.

As difficult as it may be, and believe me, I've had my moments of biting my tongue until it is double in size, try to keep your anger away from the kids. Call a friend, a relative, a hot line, a counselor, or anyone just to vent, but don't vent to the children.

Unlike my advice to men to reveal the information to your wife as soon as possible, when it comes to the children, there are some times that are better than others. It takes a lot of thought and consideration, but remember, the happiness and security of your children should always come first.

Chapter 8

Breaking up is Hard to do

In the fifteen years that I have counseled straight wives, the majority of them wanted to know why it is so hard to move on in their lives. Many of these women were paralyzed and afraid to make a move to end their miserable existence. Others were no longer in the marriages, but stuck in a maze of confusion, unable to move past the victimization phase and forward to a happier life. Let's discuss the causes of this problem and some solutions to show how to move forward.

Keep in mind, I did not end my marriage. My ex-husband walked out in anger hoping that this would force me into further submission allowing him to do as he pleased. If Michael did not leave, I doubt that I would have done anything to hasten the breakup. I was part of a syndrome that so many women fall into when they are emotionally or physically abused. Although my ex-husband never lifted a hand to me or physically threatened me, I was mentally beaten beyond recognition. I used to criticize women who stayed in abusive marriages prior to that time, but I have since learned not to judge anyone's inability to walk away.

When I married Michael, I was a strong and independent woman. Within four years, I was a stranger to myself, my family, and friends who couldn't figure out what had happened to me. This is typical of so many of the women I have worked with. Living with someone who is consciously or unconsciously ripping away each layer of your self-esteem on a daily basis takes its toll on your sense of confidence and ability to think.

When women suspect or learn that their husbands are gay or "bisexual," they usually start blaming themselves because they don't understand homosexuality. "If only I was a better wife...if only I was better in bed...if only I was less demanding...if only I was more attractive, if only I was a better housekeeper, if only I was smarter, if only, if only, if only..."

All of these "if only's" only add to our list of why we feel that we are failures in the marriage. Most of us don't understand that this is not about us—it's about them. It's about our husbands' refusals to be honest with us and even with themselves. It's about placing the blame of the failed marriage where it correctly belongs—not transferring the blame to the unsuspecting wife to avoid honesty and responsibility. It is easier to fault the wife for the problems in the marriage rather than accept homosexuality as the cause of the problems.

Ending a marriage, even a bad marriage, is difficult at best. When you lack the self-confidence that usually results from these relationships, you are scared to make a move in any positive direction. I always advise women not to give up hope even when they believe it is impossible to escape. Map out a plan in your mind—short term. Don't worry about where you want to be years from now; organize a six-month or one-year plan. Be realistic. Accept that your bad marriage needs to end and map out the steps to do it at a pace that is convenient for you. If you believe that you are stuck with no choice, you lose all hope and just give up. Stop worrying about ways to keep a destructive marriage together and instead start thinking of the steps you need to take to live without your husband. Stop trying to force something to work that is not workable.

Millions of marriages with straight couples end in divorce, and women are able to begin relationships again without the added complications of straight/gay marriages. Why is it so much harder for us to move forward? There are several reasons.

1.   THE SELF-ESTEEM ISSUE

Consciously or subconsciously, most wives blame themselves for their husbands' homosexuality, especially in the early stages of disclosure. It takes a full understanding of homosexuality to realize that in no way whatsoever are they responsible. When women learn that their husbands are gay, on some level they believe it was their failure that they were unable to "turn their husbands straight" or fulfill the needs of their husbands so those gay impulses would disappear. They continue to think the fault is theirs. After all, their husbands married them in good faith publicly committing to a lifetime of marriage, family, and all the trappings that go along with the American dream. Their husbands made the choice to be in a marriage, have sexual relations, and proclaim their love. They "chose" to lead the straight life but somewhere along the way changed their minds. If men can have a "normal" life, why would they decide to act on their homosexual impulses? They acted happy when they got married, so why couldn't they remain happy?

When a woman believes that she is responsible for her husband turning to the opposite sex for physical and emotional pleasure, how much of a woman can she be? As long as a woman feels that she was the cause of her husband's sexual reversal, she will think that she can cause this to happen again in future relationships.

SOLUTION:

First, accept the fact that your husband was gay long before you came into the picture. He has no choice in his sexuality, and you had no influence as to when he would be able to accept and deal with it—if ever. Stop cluttering your mind with the "if only" syndrome. There is only one "if only" that could make a difference—"If only you were born with a penis." Other than this, there is nothing humanly possible that you can do to change the situation.

Next, try to remember who you were before the marriage. Dig deep into your memory and start making a list of all of your positive qualities and abilities, hopes, dreams, and aspirations that were and had before this relationship. Keep looking at them each day to remember who you really are, not what you have become because of this marriage.

Start rebuilding your self-esteem by doing things for yourself. Most women become so trapped during these marriages that they are afraid to do anything that will upset the delicate balance of existing day-to-day rather than living life and finding happiness. Look for something that will enhance your self-improvement such as returning to school, getting a job, showcasing your creative abilities, writing in a journal expressing your real feelings, or making new friends. Many women cut themselves off from a social and family life fearing they will be criticized or blamed by others. This is the right time to return to the support system you had before the marriage.

I suggest that women look for support groups that deal with women's issues if they are having difficulty moving forward on their own. If there is a support group for straight/gay marriages in your community, check it out. Make sure it is not one of those groups which urges you to stay in your marriage and accept it. In the next chapter, I will explain how to find or start these groups. If there are no organizations in your area for straight/gay marriages, join a women's group that focuses on self-esteem building, assertiveness training, and positive reinforcement. Some women need to see a professional therapist to help unravel the hurt inside that doesn't seem to go away. Don't be afraid to get this help. It can make a difference in your mental health and happiness, as well as your children's, in the years ahead.

2. THE LACK OF TRUST ISSUE

There are two issues here. The first is the lack of trust in your own judgement. After all, you were the one who married your husband thinking that he was straight. How could you have been so wrong? Why didn't you pick up the signs? How do you know that you won't make this mistake again? If you didn't know the first time, how can you be sure you'll know the next time around?

SOLUTION:

The chances are, it won't happen again. After reading this book, you have enough information to know what to look for as signs of a gay male. Keep reflecting on your own marriage and the signals that something was wrong. Check any stories that have inconsistencies when anticipating a new relationship. Don't ignore them for the sake of love. This is a good practice not only in for people coming out of a straight/gay marriage, but any kind of destructive marriage. Don't find yourself in a desperate situation where you are willing to settle for anyone who knows how to say, "I love you," just because you need to hear it. Avoid rushing into a relationship because of social or financial pressures.

After Michael left, I had no financial resources and went on welfare for three years. I had two young children and I was emotionally out of synch. I took that time to repair myself mentally, go to college, earn my degrees, and move on to a happier life. I struggled financially for a long time, but I had peace of mind because each night when I went to bed, I knew that I could wake up the next day and think about a future. Throughout my marriage, I often went to bed crying because I was miserable and woke up the same way. I existed day to day—I wasn't living.

It took me many years to trust myself enough to think about a relationship again. Each of us moves at a different pace. Some women make the drastic mistake of jumping into a relationship much too fast. They don't end up with a gay husband, but they could end up with the wrong husband or relationship. Give yourself time to reconnect with who you are first. Learn that you can function independently as a person. Start rebuilding those torn away layers of self-esteem you had before the marriage, or in some cases, start building the self-esteem you lacked before the marriage.

Don't listen to the well-meaning advice of those around you who keep pressuring you to find a man again. There are people who still believe you can't be happy in life until you are a couple with someone. They will try to set you up with their friends, family members, co-workers, etc. because they believe this is the only way you can be happy. Don't be afraid to say that you are not ready to meet someone because you need time to work on yourself and resolve the issues to make you complete again. Most of us in this situation are used to being "people pleasers," meaning that our need to make others happy comes before our need to make ourselves happy. This is a red-flag sign of low personal self-esteem.

The other trust issue is the one of being able to trust a man again. Throughout the marriage to your gay husband, you were lied to, cheated on, blamed for things that were not your fault, and led to believe that you were the cause of the problems in the marriage. Is this a general trend in all men? How do you know that the next man won't do the same things to you?

SOLUTION:

Certainly this is a more difficult problem to answer. Finding a good man is a universal problem—not exclusive to ex-wives of gay men. I have counseled straight couples over the years who had bad marriages and/or relationships. There are numerous variables that determine the success of any relationship. There are no guarantees through the years no matter how certain you are about someone being the right mate at any time in your life.

The one encouraging piece of information I can tell you is that I do know couples who have wonderful marriages. These are marriages where trust is developed at an early stage and continually worked on. Every couple has its shares of arguments and problems, but that is human nature. It doesn't mean that you don't love a person or can't trust a person when this happens. No two people are identical, and to think that you can find someone who will always agree with you about everything is unrealistic and not what a caring relationship is about—it's what a controlling relationship is about!

Look for someone who shares your value systems. Never take a relationship for granted by assuming it will remain intact. It needs nurturing at all times. Don't be afraid to say, "I love you," or to express what your needs and desires are—including sexually. Talk to couples who have solid marriages and see what makes them successful. I always like to ask these couples how they keep their relationship happy and their love growing. It gives me inspiration to see that relationships can work. It's wonderful to see how positive a relationship can stay when both partners think about the needs of each other—not just one partner wondering how to please the other one.

3.   THE SEX ISSUE

The most difficult challenge for me personally was to have sex after the end of my marriage. Any kind of sexual confidence or enjoyment I had in the past seemed to fade from my memory. I felt like a sexual failure even when I knew that I was not responsible for my ex-husband's homosexuality. I was afraid to try again. I thought that I would be a disappointment to any man like I was to him. Some women jump right into the water just to start believing in themselves again sexually. Others block it from their minds like I did until the timing is right.

SOLUTION:

Trust me when I tell you that making love with someone you care about or love is the most wonderful experience in the world. I know because I have been blessed with this for the past six years after waiting over a decade after my marriage to find it. You don't have to wait until you fall in love again—you can have great sex with someone whom you feel a physical attraction to and when the chemistry is right. This can help to reassure you that you are a "normal" woman—not a nymphomaniac or bad sex partner as your gay husband led you to believe.

Although sex is not the most important factor in a relationship, it is a very important one because it builds on the intimacy in a relationship. Without it, you may as well be living with a brother or cousin. Some women are willing to settle for that, but remember, you are settling. I say you deserve more.

For many of us, having sex for the first time after our marriages was a frightening step to take because of our fear of failure. It is no surprise that if a woman has an unfulfilling sexual experience with the next man in her life, she personalizes it as her fault. After coming out of a marriage where you were led to believe that unfulfilling sex was your fault, it is understandable. We forgot, or in some cases of sexual inexperience never knew, that not every straight man is a great lover or is interested in pleasing a woman. There are plenty of men who are only interested in pleasing themselves, and they assume that you are feeling just as good as they are at the end of the encounter or they just don't care. Practice communicating with your partner that you are not satisfied just because he is. Women by nature are not assertive, and expressing your sexual needs is one of the most difficult obstacles. It took me years of bad sexual experiences to be able to say, "This is what makes me happy." If you have a responsive lover, he will remember this. If you have a lover who overlooks this or doesn't care—well, forget him and cut your losses. You've already paid your dues with unfulfilling sex in your marriage.

4. **THE ISSUE OF ACCEPTING YOUR EX-HUSBAND'S GAY LIFESTYLE WHEN THERE ARE CHILDREN INVOLVED.**

When a straight marriage ends, there can be complications resulting from the husband's new choice in companionship. The ex-wife wonders if the new woman will treat her children with kindness during the visitations and if they will accept a new woman in her husband's life. For ex-wives of gay men, the issues are far more complicated. Many women are petrified by the thought of the children being exposed to the homosexual lifestyle. Although most ex-wives eventually accept that homosexuality is not a choice that a man consciously makes because it is not a matter of choice, it doesn't mean that they are any more comfortable facing the situation. The emotions run very high here ranging from the fear that the children will somehow be influenced by the gay lifestyle to the fear that the male children will be physically molested by the gay friends or lover of the ex-husband.

There is always a fear of the unknown. To many women, the only thing they know about homosexuality is that it wrecked their marriage, and they don't want to give it a chance to destroy their children. Society promotes the message that homosexuality is perverted, distorted, and deviant.

How can women come to terms with their children around this lifestyle?

SOLUTION:

I wish I had a clear-cut answer for this problem, but I don't. The best advice I can give you is to try to communicate with your ex-husband about what is best for the children. In many of my counseling experiences, the gay husband understands the need for the children not to have to his lifestyle displayed because it creates confusion. There are so many factors to consider here including the age of the children, the location of the family, the acceptance of homosexuality by the woman, and the financial and emotional support given by the gay father.

I was fortunate that my ex-husband was careful around our children not to expose them to situations that they were too young to understand. As they grew older, I was the one who revealed the information at a time that I felt it was necessary. Michael was very angered by this because he didn't want them to know, or at least to find out from me. Children today are far more educated and perceptive about these issues than we were growing up. I did not want them to be confused by mixed messages. As they grew older, they were like most kids and natural curiosity led them to rummage through gay books and films hidden in Michael's home. They started asking me questions, and although I avoided answering directly for as long as possible, there came a time when I knew they had to know the truth. I explained the situation with great sensitivity, thought, and compassion, but when Michael found out, it caused a rift that lasted nearly a year.

I don't regret making that choice because as I explained in an earlier chapter, sexuality during adolescence is confusing under any circumstances. I also knew from doing research that the chances of having a gay child with one gay parent were higher due to genetics. I never wanted my children to ever feel self-hating or confused about themselves if this turned out to be the case.

Many women fear that their children will be psychologically damaged when they find out about the father's homosexuality. If handled correctly by both parties, this doesn't have to happen. Gay fathers need to understand that it took them years to come to terms with their homosexuality, and now that they have, they can't expect the children or wife to deal with it at the moment they can accept it.

There are some wonderful gay role models in society, and I suggest that you start finding some of those whom your children can relate to whether they are writers, musicians, actors, scientists, sports figures, or politicians. Don't dwell on the sensationalism of homosexuality that creates the stereotype that society magnifies as being typical.

You can learn about the gay community without immersing yourself in it. Too much exposure in this case can cloud your judgment and jade your opinion. You can be accepting and understanding of a different lifestyle without judging it. The gay world is different than the straight world. Values are different in some respects, but in other cases, the same. Bottom line—gay people want the same things that straight people want—to find love, happiness, and a sense of self-worth in a society that will always suffer from homophobia.

The one thing I do know is that being around gay people will not change the sexual orientation of your children. If you fear that gay is "contagious," stop thinking it. Your children have no more chance of becoming gay from being in the company of gay people than they have of becoming a different color from socializing with people of a different color. The gay community does not proselytize or prey on straight boys to become gay. Individuals may fantasize or express their desires to be with a straight male, but in most cases that's where it ends. Pedophilia is far more prevalent in the straight community than it is in the gay community. The irresponsible actions of individuals cannot be held against the community any more than the actions of individuals of any group of people.

When men in the gay community proclaim they are "proud to be gay," this is a statement of self-worthiness rather than a conscious effort of conversion to a lifestyle. Like all oppressed minorities, gay people are looking for acceptance—first by themselves, then of others.

Keep in mind when it comes to children, the security of the child feeling loved by both parents is foremost in importance. Make every effort to keep the gay father involved in the lives of the children. Positive parenting should be the main issue—not the sexuality. When either party loses sight of this, the children are the real losers.

All of this is good advice, but sometimes you have a father who is not cooperative in communicating with you and doesn't care about your feelings or your children's feelings of discomfort. As I mentioned in an earlier chapter about the actions of a leader of the Gay Father's Coalition who insisted on taking his son to gay outings, marches, and picnics, do what you have to do to protect your child from feeling uncomfortable. You do have rights as the mother, and in most cases, the primary caretaker, to fight for the well-being of your child's mental health. If this means taking the issue to court, then do it.

Chapter 9

Bisexuality—Illusion and Delusion

I hear it all the time and I've heard it for years. "My husband is not *gay*, he is *bisexual*." Or, I hear from the husbands that, "There's no way I am gay; I have bisexual tendencies." When I first started counseling wives and straight/gay couples, I would get angry when those words would start the conversation after the informal pleasantries. I was in the beginning stages of my own recovery, and my anger from the lies and deceit of my ex-husband during our marriage was still too fresh in my mind. But now, years later, I can calmly discuss this issue with objectivity and understanding because most of my pain and anger is gone. I do admit, though, that the whole issue still irritates me.

Let's talk reality. What is bisexuality anyway? A married gay man who has sex with his wife but still sexually desires a man? A man who lives a straight life with a wife and children to shield him in public while he has homosexual encounters on the side? A man who claims he is attracted to both men and women but still needs a man when he's with a woman? I think not.

Bisexuality is an excuse. For gay men it is an illusion, creating a picture that allows them to fit into the straight world. For their straight wives it is a delusion, creating a justification for keeping the marriage together.

If straight/gay couples choose to keep their marriage together for whatever reasons, that is a choice they make. But the problem with using bisexuality as the justification only postpones the inevitable of facing the real issue. I say this at the beginning rather than the end because it is important to keep this thought in mind while you sift through the following discussion.

First, let's look at the overall picture. Most women don't understand homosexuality. I didn't. I thought a gay person is attracted to someone of the same sex. That's what I learned from an early age, and no one disputed those facts. Yes, I heard about movie stars that married and turned out to be gay. But those were Hollywood stories, and in the movies, anything goes. It did-n't have any sense of reality to me. I recognized gay people once I reached my mid-to-late teens. Everyone could identify them because they always stood out. The gay guys were effeminate and flamboyant. They always had girl friends around them, but no girlfriends. Girls loved them because they were wonderful confidants, advice givers, and fashion experts. They would gossip with you, help you fashion your hair, and confirm whether or not your choice in men would have been their choice.

And we never understood what made men gay, we only knew it was wrong. We couldn't visualize two men being passionate together like we were with the men we fell in love with. We could intellectualize it, but we couldn't imagine it without thinking there was something sick and demented about it. There was no way we could ever suspect that we could marry someone gay and not know it.

So how did it happen? How could something that seemed so clear become so jumbled and confusing? How could our judgment be so off-target? Easy. It was our misconception of "gay." We didn't know that there were gay men who had the ability to perform sexually with a woman even though it was certainly not a preference. Not all gay men can do this, but some can. Does it mean they want to have sex with a woman? Not really. Given the choice, they are not going to pick you. But the problem is, those gay men who can perform with women believe they don't have a choice.

These men are caught between two worlds and are really lost. They are emotionally straight, but physically gay. They don't emotionally fit into the gay world, and they are hoping that their ability to perform heterosexually will take away the nagging physical attraction they have for men. They can't come to terms with themselves because they too have been taught that there is something morally wrong with being gay. And so they live a lie, living it with you and resenting you for it. They misplace their own frustrations on their wives and express it through anger and hostility where it hurts the most.

Some husbands do come to terms with their homosexuality at some point, but there is no way to predict when this will happen. A year, two, ten, twenty, forty—I've seen it take place at all different times. But many married gay men are never able to give up the comfort and safety of living in the straight world, even if it isn't quite as comfortable as they would like it to be. The challenge alone of finding ways to avoid sexual relations with your wife has to be exhausting. No matter how difficult living a lie may be, it is easier than being part of the gay world. How do they know that? Because they have explored the gay world, even if it is from a distance. They tested the waters, putting in one toe at a time, never able to submerge the whole foot.

The gay world wasn't something they could identify with—it was a bunch of freaks who blatantly bragged to the outside world that they were proud of this fluke. It lacked sincerity, commitment and depth. Everything was focused on one thing—sex. They saw public displays at the gay bars where men embraced each other and passionately kissed. They watched men dancing together and grinding their bodies in a lewd manner. They were approached by young male prostitutes on the streets in gay neighborhoods offering all kinds of sexual services for money. They read the gay newspapers and looked through the personal ads which may have sexually excited them but emotionally repulsed them. And what they saw, they hated. They were overcome with a sense of shame and revulsion. This was definitely not who they were. And so they ran back to the safety net. They ran home to their marriage, thinking of ways to fulfill those deepening urges without revealing their identity.

At some point, these men find the opportunity to act on their homosexual needs and they think it's okay. Why? Because they're not gay—merely "bisexual." Big deal. What does it have to do with you anyway? It's not like they're cheating on you with another woman. You should feel better about that. Don't take it personally. It's just a character flaw that you can learn to live with. If you really love your husband, you should be willing to overlook his little male indiscretions and his occasional weaknesses that he has no control over.

And then there is you, the wife who finally learns what is ripping apart your self-esteem day by day. Now it all makes sense. Your husband is bisexual. You were worried it was another woman. You may have even suspected that your husband was homosexual. What a relief! Here you thought divorce was looming overhead for reasons unknown but now you know that this is a workable problem. Bisexual. You have a fighting chance to make the marriage work. Right? Wrong!

When my ex-husband alluded to being "bisexual" during one (and only one) conversation in our marriage, I wasn't exactly stunned. There were hints building up over time that pointed me in that direction, so it was somewhat of a relief when he didn't blow up or dispute my accusation. Bisexual. It sure sounded and felt much better than "homosexual" which was my greatest fear. I could work with "bisexual" because it meant I had a chance of pulling my husband over the middle line to my side of the fence. All I had to do was make myself into the dream wife that would make him forget about looking elsewhere. I could take away those twinges of desire he felt for men by becoming more attractive and loving. And I justified that I could live with this problem as long as it was under my terms and conditions. In the spirit of compromise necessary in every good marriage, I made my list.

If you have to go out every six months or so to take care of your business, I can live with it.

As long as you satisfy whatever needs you have with someone of consenting age, I can live with it.

As long as I never have to know anything about this phase of your life, I can live with it.

I had it all wrapped up in a neat package. My husband gave my conditions a nod of acceptance, and we stated that we would never discuss it again.

Of course, this agreement was pushing me even further into the state of delusion. Once I knew that my husband wanted to have sex with men, it didn't matter what the classification of his sexuality was. I started obsessing and panicking every time he walked out the door without an explanation. Was this going to be the day? Who was he with? If he was bisexual, why couldn't I satisfy his needs? That's the problem. Intellectually we can filter the information that we are not at fault, but when your husband engages in sex with a man, emotionally we don't believe it. Although your husband justifies to himself that it's not cheating because it's a man, after a while you can't. Infidelity is infidelity. Cheating is cheating. Do you feel better that he's bestowing his passion on a man—the passion he's never had for you?

I was scared and nervous once I faced the truth. I didn't want to break up my marriage. I loved my husband even though he treated me with contempt. I could never do anything right in his eyes because subconsciously, I stood between him and his happiness. I was cramping his style, but as time went on, he grew bolder and stopped caring about what I thought. Throughout our marriage, my husband denied being gay. After our "bisexual agreement," he denied admitting to anything; he claimed he just went along with my paranoid thoughts to placate me. By this time it was harder to fool me. I knew the signs like the glances at attractive young men that lasted far too long or the camaraderie with males that far exceeded the boundaries of friendship.

After the breakup of my marriage, my husband was able to jump into the water full force and tried to find his place in the gay world. He wasn't sure where he belonged although he had been physically part of that world for years before I met him. He had a love/hate relationship with the gay community. He knew what he wanted sexually, but found the gay lifestyle empty. The straight lifestyle offered him a security blanket. A loving wife, adorable children, respectability, stability—who wouldn't want that? For gay men who marry, they believe they can have the best of both worlds—the American dream plus an extra dream on the side. But at what expense to that devoted wife who trusts him to be honest and faithful?

Believe me, I am sympathetic to women who are scared to face the truth. I was one of them, and it was the most difficult struggle I've ever dealt with. My ground rules of what I could live with kept changing as my husband became bolder and less secretive. And each time I had to modify those ground rules to his advantage, I became more broken down mentally because I was giving in to something that I couldn't accept—a way of life that was unacceptable in a marriage. The worst part was that I believed it was *my* personal failure. If my husband was bisexual, I must be doing something wrong or otherwise he would want to be with me instead of a man.

Most gay men are wonderful to their wives when they feel an overpowering sense of guilt for their indiscretions. They are not looking to intentionally hurt their wives, and much like the abuse syndrome, all kinds of promises of change and reform are made when they are caught. It's like the honeymoon is starting all over again, giving the wife a false sense of desperately needed hope. The husband becomes loving, giving, and even semi-passionate for a time to prove that his little mistake is in the past and should be forgiven and forgotten. But it usually doesn't take long before the big pull starts. That's just the way it is when nature takes its course. And each time it happens, the wife becomes more alert to the warning signs and can almost anticipate what's around the corner when her husband leaves the house.

It all comes down to what you are willing to live with. If your husband is having sex with men, you can call it whatever name you want, but as the old saying goes, a rose by any other name is still a rose. A man who has sexual relations with a man is still a gay man in my book. And a final warning for those of you whose husbands keep reassuring you that they have these gay attractions but never acted on them. Don't believe it. In almost all cases, they have acted on their needs either prior to or during your marriage. They may claim that they are just watching gay porno movies or reading gay magazines to satisfy these urges, but that's usually a ploy to make you feel better and throw you off track.

I have met hundreds of gay husbands in marriages, leaving marriages, and after their marriages. At some point during their marriages, most of them were having gay sex in one form or another through casual dating, one-night stands, or full-fledged relationships and lying to their wives to "protect" their marriages. We desperately want to believe the lies they tell us. Even when the truth is smacking us right in the face, we believe their excuses because the truth is too painful to accept. We build a layer in our subconscious that I refer to as "limbo"—a state of mind where we exist day to day without living life because we are hurting too badly. And some women are able to live their lives this way indefinitely rather than give themselves the chance at real happiness and fulfillment. I understand this. Sometimes we are so mentally weakened from dealing with this horrific situation that we feel unable to stand up and make a change. Certainly I am not one to judge when a woman is ready, if ever, to make that move. I don't know if I would have had the courage and confidence to make that choice if my ex-husband didn't make it for me. When you lose all of your self-confidence and self-worth, it's hard to believe that you even deserve a chance at happiness. And so you walk through the days and nights sitting in limbo waiting for a miracle because you don't have the strength to realize that you can walk away from this trap.

The only way you will ever regain any of your mental strength back is to stop making excuses for your husband's gay behavior by labeling it "bisexual." Look at things for what they are and don't let him tell you otherwise. If he wants to keep fooling himself, fine, but don't let him keep fooling you. Each day that you can say, "my husband is gay," you will find yourself growing stronger because you can look at your marriage for what it is—not what it's not or not what you wish it could be. Only then will you be able to start thinking about the right move for yourself, your future, and your long-deserved happiness in the world of the living, not the world of existing.

Chapter 10

Starting over

As a postscript, I want to leave you, the reader, with a strong sense of hope and optimism. Not a false sense, but a genuine feeling that life will move ahead when you allow it to do so. I love hearing from women whose lives I have touched over the years who found real happiness the next time around when they met the mates they needed and deserved. Of course, not all of the stories had a "happily ever after" ending. Those women who didn't learn from the mistakes of their marriages to their gay husbands often found themselves in the wrong relationships again under different circumstances. This is why it is so important to realize that you need the time to rebuild yourself and find happiness within yourself without depending on someone else to make you feel worthy.

I took the time I needed to do this, and the investment paid off. Excusing the use of a cliché, I "followed my dreams" by returning to school and earned my degrees in counseling. I raised my children as a single parent facing the challenges of juggling work, family, friends, and personal time alone. I made plenty of mistakes along the way, but I tried to learn from each one of them so I wouldn't repeat them. I learned to trust and love again, but that was after I felt whole as a person. I am still faced daily with new adversities to overcome, but I guess that's what makes you appreciate the good times in life that much more. I take nothing for granted—I look at each new day as an adventure in living.

When my marriage ended, I felt isolated and alone. There was virtually nowhere to turn, so I started my own support group. As I mentioned earlier, I started the support group to be just that— a group that would support people in straight/gay marriages regardless of the status of the marriage. As time went on, that changed when I saw how self-defeating these marriages were for the wives who existed in a state of acceptance for their husbands' needs. In good conscience, I was unable to support couples who wanted to stay together and work it out. Since neither partner could ever be really happy, it was a lose-lose situation. What's the point in advocating a losing situation?

Over the years, some women who were angered by my stance have come back to me and told me that I was right— there was no way the marriages could work. I didn't feel any sense of happiness in their admitted defeat. I am never one to say, "I told you so," because who am I to judge the rate of acceptance that it takes someone to realize they are trapped in their own insecurities, if ever.

Each of us has to find the way out of this tangled maze at her own pace. Each of us has be able to have the strength to move ahead, making our own timetable and not being influenced by the outside pressures that so often get in the way. These pressures can be from family, religious beliefs, well-meaning friends, counselors, or the misguided advice from some support groups that make you feel that if you can't keep the marriage together, you are the failure.

When looking for support in this area, there are places to turn. How do you start to find the proper resources? My most important message to you before starting this search is to remember that there are groups all over this country that may not meet your needs. If this is the case, retreat immediately—don't become more confused by a message that is uncomfortable to you. Keep looking and if you still can't find the help you are looking for, consider starting your own group that will work for you. In the chapter on how I started my group, SOGA, I gave you information about the founding of the group and you can follow that lead. For step-by-step directions, feel free to write or email me and I will send you a kit on starting a support group.

There is one support group that I have found on line named St8 Spouses of Lesbians and Gays. The symbol of the group is the butterfly, which is found throughout the Web page. Jean Copeland, the founder of the group, states, "The butterfly represents the metamorphosis we undergo...from chrysalis to butterfly. The cocoon represents the unmet needs from a dysfunctional relationship and the stifling of who we are. The butterfly represents the freedom we find to fly and land where we choose, freedom from the bonds that kept us from being who we want to be, free from unmet needs which controlled us, finding the fulfillment that we all long for in our lives." Jean has allowed me to share information about her AOL on-line group with you.

In Jean's own words, she explains:

When I first confirmed my suspicions that my husband was gay after 26 years of marriage, I immediately sought support to no avail. This only added to my feelings of isolation

and thinking I was the only person this had ever happened to.
A few months later in the summer of 1996, a support message
board for straight spouses of gays and lesbians was created on
America On Line. In the intervening years it has grown from
an original six people posting there to a huge online network
where thousands have found support. It has become a lifeline
to many—a place where straight spouses of gay and lesbian
partners share common issues, receive recovery support,
exchange topical resources and freely express personal experiences, such as impact issues upon children, friends, family,
and social environment.

Our commonality transcends our diverse backgrounds,
varying geographic locations and individual circumstances.
In sharing this common issue, we create a comfort zone
which allows us as a group to reinforce each other, validate
our experience and draw emotional sustenance from one
another. It is through having a safe haven to vent feelings
and share experiences that we help one another learn to
cope, deal, heal and eventually rebuild. One of the advan-
tages of an online group is instant access to others when one
feels a need to connect, and just from our sheer numbers one
will find another whose situation parallels their own, one
with whom one can totally relate.

I have maintained a list of all who have sought support
and created a referral list to allow people to connect in their
local areas with others sharing this issue. While many find
the online support helpful, particularly since one can maintain anonymity if that is important to them, many of us
have found face-to-face local support to be even more valuable. Many lasting friendships have blossomed from this

group. We often find we are kindred spirits, sharing more than just this common issue. The creation of some local support chapters for straight spouses has resulted from this networking for support on AOL.

In addition to the message board, we also have two weekly support chats. One is a hosted two-hour chat on Mondays for all straight spouses, and the other is a private room chat on Tuesdays for still married only. While we have many common issues, we do have issues unique to divorce or staying married. Needless to say, most mixed sexual orientation marriages do not survive long term so the majority of those in our support group are separating/divorcing. However, usually when one first seeks support one is still in the marriage. Having participants in varying stages of discovery and healing and having the diversity of people who have chosen different routes of resolution widen our scope and strengthen the support network.

It is been our observation that we start this journey thinking it is all about them (the gay spouses) only to realize somewhere along the way that it is about US. Regardless of how we resolve this issue in our lives, it brings change to all of us. Nothing remains the same. But we do find that after the initial feelings of being totally overwhelmed by the revelation of finding out we have a gay partner, as we begin to search for answers we begin to realize the answers lie within each of us. This is a time of great personal growth, and that alone results ultimately in more gains than losses. It is a time to educate oneself as to what one is dealing with, seek support and validation of one's feelings from others sharing this issue, seek professional advice from an attorney to review your options and rights, seek medical counsel to gain peace of mind that you do not have health issues as a result of unwittingly exposing yourself with your gay partner, and seek counseling (both individual and joint) to help you sort through your feelings and helping your partner to come to terms with his/her orientation. We find in addition to doing all of this, one needs to start to focus inwardly. Take care of you first and foremost. Learn to nurture yourself as you have nurtured others. Learn to love yourself and know that the gay issue has nothing to do with you or anything you did, said or are. Begin to focus on your needs, wants and goals and figure out what you can and cannot live with. Stay within your comfort zones. It's okay to draw boundary lines for your partner. As you get in touch with the inner you, you will more than likely rediscover a you that was lost somewhere along the way in a dysfunctional relationship. You will learn that you are responsible for your own happiness…it cannot come from someone else. Find your own happiness within; seek what brings you fulfillment as a person. Don't look at the door closing behind you or you might miss the doors that are now opening for you. Our life is what we make it. Learn to act for yourself rather than re-act to someone else. Put yourself in the driver's seat of your life. To allow yourself to be a passenger in a runaway vehicle only sets you up for a crash. Take control of your life. Seek resources to educate yourself as to what you are dealing with, get in touch with you and your feelings and needs, nurture yourself, seek professional counsel and the support of others sharing this painful journey, and give yourself time to work through the emotions and resolution,

remembering there is a light at the end of this dark tunnel.
Our lives are what we make it...make your life what you
want it to be.
Online Support Resources:
Straight Spouse Support Resources
http://members.aol.com/foxed/page/index.htm
For further info about the America On Line support group, con-
tact Foxed@aol.com.

I greatly commend Jean's efforts to maintain this wonderful project of supplying continuing support for women who are faced with their husbands' homosexuality. This site is a lifeline for those who need help not only during the discovery phase, but also throughout the transition of moving ahead. The Web site is also filled with other valuable information such as legal, health and additional resources advice.

If you do not have access to a computer and would like to get in touch with the St8 Spouses group for resources in your area, write to me at the address listed at the end of the chapter and I will forward your request to Jean.

I am happy to share my thoughts and input with those of you who need help and guidance through email, letters, or telephone. As part of my appreciation for buying *Is He Straight?* I am offering a free counseling session by phone or email to anyone who needs it. Just fill in the coupon at the end of the book and return it to the address listed on the coupon, and I will set up a time to talk or correspond with you.

Free Counseling Certificate

This certificate entitles the bearer to one free block of counseling time with Bonnie Kaye or one of her trained counseling specialists. Counseling block is 20 minutes by telephone or email. All sessions must be reserved in advance. Client must assume cost of long distance phone charges. To reserve your free block of time, you can do one of the following:

1. Email Bonnie Kaye at BonKaye @aol.com

or

2. Send a request for counseling time to:
   Bonnie Kaye, M.Ed.
   PMB 322
   8001 Castor Avenue
   Philadelphia, PA 19152

A time that is agreeable to both parties will be arranged as quickly as possible.